CULTURES OF THE WORLD®
DAGESTAN

Edward Beliaev & Oksana Buranbaeva

MARSHALL CAVENDISH BENCHMARK

NEW YORK

PICTURE CREDITS
Cover: © Karol Kallay / Bilderberg / Peter Arnold Inc.
Bes Stock: 7, 50, 86, 131 • Boyny, Michael / Stockfood: 127 • The Bridgeman Art Library: 14,
20, 23 • Camera Press: 32, 105 • Corbis, Inc.: 85 • Eye Ubiquitous / Hutchison Library: 65,
102 • Getty Images: 16, 49, 53, 54, 65, 114, 116, 119, 121 • HBL Network: 28 • Hutchison
Library: 8, 46, 52, 55, 56, 57, 58, 61, 77, 79, 99, 122 • Lonely Planet Images: 51 • Novosti: 43,
94, 129 • Novosti / TopFoto: 50, 73 • Reuters: 30, 35, 36, 53, 90, 109 • Topham Picturepoint:
130 • Travel Images: 1, 3, 4, 5, 6, 9, 10, 11, 12, 13, 18, 38, 40, 45, 59, 63, 66, 69, 70, 74, 80,
82, 87, 88, 92, 96, 101, 106, 108, 110, 112, 113, 115, 124 • Wikimedia: 25

ACKNOWLEDGMENTS
The authors wish to thank Rimma Buranbaeva for her research assistance.

PRECEDING PAGE
The staff of a rural school on a Saturday outing in the Dagestani village of Agvali.

Marshall Cavendish Benchmark
99 White Plains Road
Tarrytown, NY 10591
Website: www.marshallcavendish.us

© Marshall Cavendish International (Asia) Private Limited 2006
® "Cultures of the World" is a registered trademark of Times Publishing Limited.

Series concept and design by Times Editions
An imprint of Marshall Cavendish International (Asia) Private Limited
A member of Times Publishing Limited

All Internet sites were correct and accurate at the time of printing.

Library of Congress Cataloging-in-Publication Data
Beliaev, Edward.
   Dagestan / by Edward Beliaev and Oksana Buranbaeva.—1st ed.
      p. cm.—(Cultures of the world)
   Includes bibliographical references and index.
   Summary: "An exploration of the geography, history, government, economy,
      people, and culture of the former Soviet republic of Dagestan"—Provided
      by publisher.
   ISBN 0-7614-2015-0
   1. Dagestan (Russia)—Juvenile literature. I. Buranbaeva, Oksana.
      II. Title. III. Series.
   DK511.D2B454 2005
   947.5'2—dc22   2005013698

Printed in China

7 6 5 4 3 2 1

CONTENTS

The minaret of a mosque rises above the rooftops of the surrounding village of Kvanada. Islam is the main religion in Dagestan, where Sunni Muslims make up more than 90 percent of the population.

A mountain lake near the village of Agvali in the Tsumada district of Dagestan.

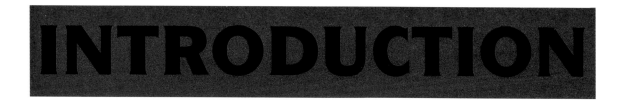

INTRODUCTION

OUTSIDE RUSSIA, LITTLE IS KNOWN about Dagestan. For those who are familiar with the republic, it is usually associated with Imam Shamil, a heroic figure who fought the Russians in the middle of the 19th century, when they entered the Caucasus Mountains. In the northern Caucasus, where Dagestan is located, the Russians' attempt to control the land met with resistance. A long and brutal war was waged for almost 40 years between the Russians and the various peoples living to the north of the main mountain chain. The most prominent participants in this conflict were the Dagestani, Chechen, and Circassian peoples.

A small but complex region, Dagestan has faced many changes in its often turbulent 3,000-year history of tribal wars and large-scale invasions. Today the country bears the influence of the many people who have passed through the region or settled there. Many different ethnic groups have set down roots in Dagestan, adding their various languages, religious beliefs, and customs to the region's vibrant culture.

GEOGRAPHY

WHILE DAGESTAN IS USUALLY DESCRIBED as a mountainous country, it is easy to forget its 329 miles (530 km) of coast on the Caspian Sea or that almost half of the country (48 percent) is flatland. Dagestan is located in the eastern part of the northern Caucasus Mountains. It is a relatively small republic, just 19,617 square miles (50,300 square km), approximately half the size of Virginia or only slightly larger than either Switzerland or the Netherlands. It is the largest of the Russian republics found in the northern Caucasus. The Caspian Sea forms the republic's boundary to the east. It shares borders with Azerbaijan and Georgia to the south and with Chechnya and Stavropol, both divisions of Russia, to the west. To the north, the Kuma River forms its border with Kalmykiya, another republic of the Russian Federation.

Left: **A sheep has strayed from its herd and stands perched on a slope in the Caucasus Mountains near where the Silk Road once passed through Dagestan.**

Opposite: **Dagestan is a region of varied and often contrasting terrain. Snow-covered peaks preside over lush valleys dotted with colorful wildflowers.**

A village sits snugly on a gentle mountain slope in Dagestan. Generations of highland Dagestanis have lived close to the land, learning how to survive in the republic's more remote regions.

FOUR REGIONS

Dagestan is usually divided into four geographic regions. Three of the regions are found in the southern part of Dagestan, a mostly mountainous area (except for a narrow strip along the Caspian Sea) that is difficult to access. The foothills include the low mountain chains that stretch in a northwest-southeast direction and are broken by wide valleys. The inner mountainous region is characterized by wide plateaus and crests of up to 8,200 feet (2,500 m), sometimes marked by plunging canyons. The most famous river canyon, the Sulak, is 2,400 feet (730 m) deep. Finally, the high mountain area is the site of two mountain chains that make up the Caucasus—the Watershed Ridge and the Lateral.

Only the northern side of the Watershed Ridge falls in Dagestan. The republic's highest point, Bazardyuze peak at 14,700 feet (4,480 m), is also found there, close to the border with Azerbaijan. There are several summits along the Watershed Ridge that exceed 13,125 feet (4,000 m). Among those in Dagestan are Dyul'tydag at 13,554 feet (4,131 m) and

Addala Shukhgelmezr reaching 13,619 feet (4,151 m). From the Watershed Ridge, the mountainous terrain stretches for 112 miles (180 km) to the north. The mountainous sectors make up 52 percent of Dagestan's entire area.

The Caspian lowlands lie to the north of the mountains. This area, together with part of Stavropol and Chechnya, is actually one large region located along the Terek and Kuma rivers. It is sometimes called the Tersko-Kumskaya lowlands. Farmers and herders moved their cattle to the lowlying pastures there in winter. The Kuma River serves as a border between Dagestan and Kalmykiya. It usually dries up by midsummer because of the irrigation canals that drain much of its water. In the

Two small mountain lakes near the Kvanada settlement in the Tsumada district of Dagestan.

A narrow river flows through a canyon in Aknada in Dagestan.

extensive delta region, marshes cover much of the area. The Terek delta, for instance, is 62 miles (100 km) wide, with a total area of 1,544 square miles (4,000 square km). West of the delta is the Nogay Steppe.

The Terek River, probably the best known of the Caucasus rivers, unrolls for 387 miles (623 km). It begins in the glaciers of the Caucasus. It flows through the high mountain terrain and gorges—including the legendary Daryal Gorge—through the territories of South Ossetia in the republic of Georgia and the northern Caucasian republics of the Russian Federation (including North Ossetia and Kabardino-Balkariya). From there, it wends its way to the foothills and plains of Ingushetiya, Chechnya, and Dagestan. As with other mountain rivers, the bulk of the water flows in spring and summer with the lowest levels coming during the fall and winter. The Terek River is connected to the Kuma River by an irrigation canal. As with other big rivers in the region, there are hydroelectric power plants along the Terek. One is in Dagestan, near the town of Kizlyar. The Terek formed the southern border of Russian settlement in the Caucasus until the 1860s.

A considerable part of the lowlands lies below the level of the Caspian Sea. Agriculture flourishes in the region. Two additional major rivers flowing through Dagestan are the Sulak and the Samur. Both flow through the mountainous areas of Dagestan. All rivers in the eastern Caucasus region flow from the mountains to the Caspian Sea. The republic's system of rivers is quite extensive. The Sulak, for example, is a grouping of rivers unto itself. It consists of the main channel of the Sulak as well as the Avarskoye Koysu, Andiyskoye Koysu, Kazikumukhskoye Koysu, and Kara Koysu. Dagestan's rivers are not navigable for large vessels but are used for hydroelectric power, as a water supply, and for transporting logs produced by the timber industry. The Sulak River alone has five

A vehicle crosses a bridge near Hvarshiny in Dagestan. Sturdy transport is often needed when navigating some of the republic's more rugged terrain.

The Sulak meteorological station is located in the Caucasus Mountains at an altitude of 9,688 feet (2,953 m).

hydroelectric power plants. Small lakes are found mostly in the lower reaches of the Terek and Sulak rivers.

Dagestan's Caspian coastline stretches for 335 miles (540 km). The sandy beaches and warm waters draw residents and visitors alike for vacationing or for therapeutic treatments at spas. One essential drawback, however, is that throughout most of the area there is not enough freshwater. Two prominent bays mark the coast. Kizlyarski Bay is located where the Kuma River flows into the Caspian Sea. Agrahanski Bay lies between the Terek River delta and the Agrahanski Peninsula. In Kizlyarski Bay, along the coast as well as on several small islands, the wildlife preserve Dagestansky Zapovednik has been established. There are several islands along the Caspian coast that belong to Dagestan. The islands Chechen and Tyuleni are among the largest.

CLIMATE

Dagestan's climate is generally mild and dry. Naturally temperatures and conditions vary considerably with the terrain. In the lowlands, winter temperatures are between -20°F and -16°F (-3°C and 3°C), but in the mountains it often reaches -23°F (-11°C). Summers are warm—up to 77°F (25°C) in July. Annual precipitation also varies from 8 to 12 inches (20 to 30 cm) in the northern lowlands to 24 to 32 inches (60 to 80 cm) in the mountains.

The soil also varies with the terrain. In the lowlands, especially in the Nogay Steppe, the soil is not ideally suited for agriculture, and farmers and herders use the region to pasture their livestock. But in the foothills, a much richer, blacker soil is found. As a result, a variety of grasses and vegetation thrives in the lowlands and partly in the low foothills.

In the higher foothills, those with an altitude of between approximately 1,640 and 4,922 feet (500 and 1500 m), there are forests with often dense stands of oak, beech, and hornbeam. In the mountains, birches and pines grow, as well as the tough, adaptable plants and low trees that live in the alpine meadows. Forests are found scattered across the country. Together they cover about 10 percent of Dagestan.

Another valuable resource is the rich reserves of oil and gas found beneath the Caspian Sea, only some of which are in Dagestani territory. These valuable substances have given rise to oil refineries and the chemical industry. Mineral resources are found in Dagestan's many mountain chains, but they are generally difficult and costly to extract due to the harsh terrain and climate.

A cave harbors ice formations in the Addala Shukhgelmezr, one of the highest peaks in the Watershed Ridge.

13

HISTORY

FOR MORE THAN 3,000 YEARS, the entire region of the northern and southern Caucasus has witnessed ongoing wars among the Caucasian tribes, as well as among the various empires that have gained and lost power in the area. The Persians, Romans, Ottomans, and Russians have all seen their fortunes rise and decline in the vast area. The region has been the subject of large-scale invasions by the Arabs, the Mongols, and the Timurs.

An independent state known as Dagestan did not exist before the territory was organized by the Soviet authorities in 1921. The Dagestan Autonomous Soviet Socialist Republic was established then as a part of the new Soviet state.

Before that time, the territory that would come to be known as Dagestan never had precise or set borders. It was populated by different tribes, some of which spoke similar languages, while others had their own dialects and tongues. Over many centuries, a wide range of peoples migrated in and out of the territory.

Because the Caucasus as a whole is a relatively small and contained region—when compared to the rest of Russia or stretches of central Asia—the groups that settled there have been closely interacting for centuries. Beginning at the end of the first millennium A.D., organized states have existed in the region. They would emerge, then collapse, and then new states would appear to replace them, often in the form of loose confederations of peoples, clans, and tribes.

Thus, the history of present-day Dagestan includes the history of the entire Caucasus region. Dagestan's ever-changing borders and its inhabitants have been influenced by forces originating both within and beyond the republic.

Opposite: **This 19th-century print depicts armies crossing the Soulak Pass in the Dagestan region.**

A group of friends
explores the perimeter
of the Derbent fortress.

ANCIENT HISTORY

Archaeologists have concluded that the territory that makes up present-day Dagestan has been continuously inhabited since the Stone Age. A narrow strip along the Caspian Sea—about 2 miles (3 km) wide near the city of Derbent, between the sea and the high mountains—served from ancient times as a migration route for many peoples as well as an access point for a series of foreign invaders. Derbent, located at a narrow gap between the sea and the mountains, was founded in A.D. 438 as a fortress to guard the important caravan route that stretched from southwestern Europe to southwestern Asia. Because this key avenue for trade passed through Dagestani territory, the area became the home of a diverse range of peoples and cultures.

The Caucasus also became one of the major routes along which technological innovations spread from Asia and the Middle East to Europe. The Caucasus itself, some historians say, was also one of the places where significant strides in the development of metallurgy were made. These innovations then spread to the outlying regions. Metalworkers initially focused on copper, later turning their attention to bronze and iron. This progression is not surprising as the Caucasus is rich in metal ores.

Early in the region's history, several tribes, including the Legues, Guels, and Utines, formed alliances. At the end of the first millennium B.C., some of these groupings united to form a large state—called Caucasian Albania—in the eastern Caucasus. Around that time, a few cities emerged in Dagestani territory, including Chola, Toprakhkala, and Urtseki.

ARABS AND PERSIANS

In the third century A.D., the Sassanids from Persia invaded the southern part of present-day Dagestan, making it all the way to the contemporary city of Derbent. A century later, the Huns captured the coastline to the north of Derbent. By the fourth century, sizable cities had emerged on the coast. Derbent, Semender, and Zerekhgeran (Kubachi) became increasingly bustling and ever-larger urban centers. Handicrafts and a sizable trade network also began to develop in the region.

From A.D. 664 Dagestan became the target of repeated invasions by the Arabs who tried to convert the tribes to Islam. The people resisted, sometimes with the help of their northern neighbor, the Khazar Khanate. In exchange, the people would assist other regions beset by Arab invaders. In 851 fighters supported the Georgian revolt against the Arabs. Then, in 905 and also from 913 to 914, the united tribes defeated the Arab-controlled vassals in Shirvan and Derbent. The Arabs, however, left a lasting mark on the region's native residents. The Arabs not only introduced them to Islam, sometimes forcibly, they also introduced their writings and handicrafts to the area.

In the middle of the 11th century, the Seljuks captured the territory that now includes Azerbaijan and a considerable part of Dagestan. But a century later, several independent states emerged in Dagestan, including the Avar Khanate, Kazikumukh Shamkhal, Utsmi of Kaitag, and other small political groupings. The repeated attempts made by these confederations to unite all of Dagestan under their rule failed. Wars and ethnic conflicts prevented the goal from being realized.

As in the past, the region became subject to continued waves of invasion. In the 1220s Dagestan was subjected to the overwhelming onslaught of the Mongols. Then, in the 14th century, the Uzbek, Tokhtamysh, and Timur armies invaded the region.

In the 16th century, especially after the Muscovite state annexed the Kazan (1552) and Astrakhan (1556) khanates, the Russians extended their area of control and influence that much closer to the territory that would become the republic of Dagestan. As a result, ties between Moscow and the people living in the region became more entwined. The Russians, to defend their southern frontier from the Ottomans and other Turkic tribes, established forts along the Terek River, the most prominent of which was Fort Terki, founded by L. Novoseltsev of Astrakhan in 1577 at the confluence of the Sunzha and Terek rivers. Then, in 1583, the fort was moved to the mouth of the Terek.

The forts served not only a military purpose but also as places of commercial exchange between the Russians and the mountain peoples. The tribes needed trade items such as grain, so they came to the plains to bargain for goods. They often exchanged sheep for grain or firearms. Cossacks had established themselves earlier in the region, by the first half of the 16th century. By the end of the century, a large number of the cossack frontiersmen lived along the Terek. The Russian government used the cossacks to defend its southern border and paid them for their services with money, grain, firearms, and munitions.

Often relations with the local tribes were friendly. The Russians, and their cossacks, formed fluid alliances with some of the tribes, helping them defend themselves from enemies. At other times, groups of opposing forces united and attacked the Russians. In this unstable political climate, some Dagestani rulers sought Russian protection. Thus, in the first half of the 17th century, the Shamkhal of Tarku, the Utsmi of Kaitag, and other peoples accepted and submitted to Russian suzerainty, in which the dominant foreign power controlled the region's foreign relations but allowed the area's leaders to oversee local and internal affairs.

In 1722 weaknesses in the Persian empire prompted Czar Peter the Great to invade the part of the eastern Caucasus controlled by the Persians. From the Volga River, Peter traveled south along the coast of the Caspian Sea to easily penetrate Persian-held territory. He was soon forced to withdraw, but, as a result of this campaign, Russia gained control, for a short time, of the western coast of the Caspian Sea. In 1735, by the terms of the Ganjin Treaty with Persia, however, Russia removed its troops from the

Opposite: **A Russian wears a traditional cossack uniform. The cossacks were known for their military prowess and played a significant role in the expansion of the Russian empire from the 17th to the 20th century.**

This 1855 lithograph by Thomas Packer presents a view of the territory Russia controlled in Europe and Asia.

coast. At the same time, in the northern Caucasus, Russia started to build a network of military settlements and forged alliances with the princes of Kabardia. This part of the region was located close to the Black Sea coast and occupied by the Ottomans.

Through the entire 18th century, Russian leaders, utilizing the speed and force of the cossacks, were actively engaged in colonizing and building a line of defense along the Terek River and farther to the west. New important fortress towns were built, among them Vladikavkas in 1784 (the present-day capital of North Ossetia) and later, in 1818, Grozny (the present-day capital of Chechnya).

In 1796, after the Persians sacked Tiflis (in present-day Georgia), the Russians occupied the Caspian coast at Derbent and forced some local khanates and free tribes to submit to their rule. In 1813, according to the terms of the Gulistan peace treaty signed by the Russians, Persia finally ceded control of those khanates along the Caspian Sea from Lenkoran (located in present-day Azerbaijan, near the border with Iran) to Derbent.

It was at that point, for the first time, that all the geographic areas that make up present-day Dagestan were under Russian ownership.

THE 19TH CENTURY

The Russians started to gain inroads into the region during the 16th century, mostly on the plains along the Terek and Kuban rivers, which flow from the mountains through the territories of Stavropol and Krasnodar to the Azov and Black seas. Relations between the Russian settlers and local tribes were usually, though not always, friendly and mutually beneficial.

In Dagestan, in the beginning of the 19th century, several khanates and free communities accepted Russian suzerainty, including the ruler of Avaria, the most important khanate in Dagestan. By the middle of the 1820s Dagestan appeared to be under the full control of Russia. Nevertheless the 19th century witnessed the most ferocious war in the northern Caucasus. Lasting for half a century, from 1817 to 1864, it started soon after Russia annexed the southern Caucasus, or the area that makes up present-day Georgia, Azerbaijan, and Armenia.

The conflict arose for various reasons. Rulers in the northern and southern Caucasus were motivated to come under Russian protection by the constant threat of strife in the region between the great regional powers—most notably the Persians, the Ottomans, and later the Russians. Interregional wars were also continuously fought among the rulers themselves and the numerous factions. To add to the complex situation, some of the rulers who submitted to Russian control would later rebel against that strong central power. Often Russia ruthlessly crushed the rebel forces and annexed their territory.

When Russia became the sole power in most of the Caucasus in the beginning of the 19th century, the need to ensure safe communication lines between Russia proper and its newly annexed territories south of the Watershed Ridge became essential. Russia felt it had to suppress unruly mountain tribes living in the northern Caucasus. These groups made frequent incursions on Russian forts and managed to disrupt communications with the Transcaucasus, south of the mountains. Economic, religious, and cultural factors also played an important role in this fight. For example, the restless advance of General A. P. Yermolov, the Russian commander in the Caucasus, through the mountainous regions of Chechnya and Dagestan forced the local population either to resettle in the flatlands under the protection of the watchful Russian garrisons or to move even farther and higher into the mountains.

Either way, this uprooting managed only to totally disrupt the way of life of the mountain people. The upheaval and lack of stability prompted some Dagestani rulers to unite against the Russians. During the first years of the uprising, they suffered nothing but defeat. The Russians then confiscated the rebels' lands or handed them over to vassals. The rebels attempted to enlist the support of the Persians and Ottomans against Russia, but it was too late. Russia had become too strong a power for them. From 1826 to 1828, Russia defeated Persia and seized control of the Yerevan and Nakhichevan khanates (in present-day Armenia and Azerbaijan respectively). Then, as a result of the 1828–29 war with the Ottoman empire, Russia acquired the Black Sea coast from the mouth of the Kuban River north to Adjaria. The extent of their holding included the forts of Akhaltsikhe and Akhalkalaki in present-day Georgia, not far from the Turkish border.

The aggression and frequent cruelty of the Russian army toward the area's native residents often led to spontaneous mass rebellions. The first happened in Chechnya in 1825. It was suppressed the following year. Then, in the late 1820s, one of the most interesting phenomena of

this period emerged. A religious movement called Muridism, which was basically a form of Sufism, had arrived in the region. A political aspect of this religious movement was added by Imam Muhammad of Ghumri, also called Ghazi Mullah. He was a Muslim leader who called for a holy war, or jihad, against the Russians. He was succeeded by Hamza Bey and then by Shamil. These imams succeeded in creating a theocratic, or religion-based, state called an imamate that existed for almost three decades, from the early 1830s to 1859.

In the 1840s the imamate occupied all of Chechnya, part of Dagestan, and parts of present-day Georgia and Azerbaijan. But it did not succeed in some territories of Dagestan. The khan of the Avars and Shamkhal of Tarku, for example, who had leaned toward Russian support, refused to recognize the suzerainty of the imam. Ghazi Mullah was killed by the Russian army during a skirmish at the village of Ghumri in 1832. Imam Hamza Bey was killed two years later by the Avars. Shamil, the third imam, was able to draw support from the Murids as well as from the

Yet another version of the legend states that Elisha Mansur was incarcerated at Schlisselburg Fortress (close to Saint Petersburg) and died there in 1794.

MURIDISM

In general, *murid* means "disciple." When applied to the Caucasus region, the term refers to a follower of a sheikh in the Islamic mystical tradition of Sufism. In the 19th century the Murids of the northeastern and north-central Caucasus (mostly Dagestan and Chechnya) were actually jihad warriors set on expelling the Russian invaders.

The history of Muridism is often associated with the somewhat mysterious figure of Elisha Mansur. Some say that he was an Italian Dominican sent by the pope to convert the Greeks of Anatolia (an area of present-day Turkey that was controlled by the Ottoman empire) to Catholicism. But he converted to Islam and was subsequently sent by the sultan to organize the Caucasian resistance against the Russians. Others say that he was a Chechen. Either way, he was able to forge a broad ethnic coalition of Muslims intent on resisting the Russians. But he was captured by the Russians and sent, in 1795, to the Solovetski monastery on the White Sea in northern Russia, approximately 124 miles (200 km) northwest of Archangel. The local monks tried to convert him to Christianity but to no avail.

Whatever the facts surrounding his life, Mansur is a legendary and heroic figure for the Chechens. His deeds had been praised by Mullah Muhammad al-Yaraghi, who was a Sufi scholar. Among his pupils were the Avars Ghazi Mullah and Shamil. Ghazi Mullah began his own preaching in 1827. The main thrust of his ministry was to encourage the Caucasian people to fully accept Islam, replacing their customary laws, which had divided them so, with Shariah laws, and ultimately to stand united against the Russians. In 1829 he spread his message throughout Dagestan. The Muslim scholars proclaimed him imam, or leader, and pledged their support for his armed struggle against the Russians and for his mission to establish Islam in the region. He was killed in 1832 in a battle.

The second imam, Hamza Bey, was killed in 1834 by his own followers. After that, Shamil, the close friend of Ghazi Mullah, became the third imam. Shamil was able to create a quasi-state, called an imamate, in the territory of present-day Chechnya and most of Dagestan. He introduced strict laws, high taxes, and an ever-increasing roster of duties. Eventually this strategy became the imamate's main problem. The long war, strict discipline, heavy tax burden, and rigorous duties (including supplying men and horses to the Murids) exhausted the people and created opposition to the Muridist regime. With the surrender of Shamil to the Russians in 1859, the imamate and the Murids ceased to exist.

Opposite: **The village of Tindi in Dagestan in the late 1890s.**

mountain peoples. Together they waged a long and often successful war against the Russians. In the end, though, the Russians prevailed, and Shamil surrendered in 1859. This conflict in the northern Caucasus is known as the Caucasian War. It lasted from 1817 to 1864. Although it was waged across the northern Caucasus and actually ended with the defeat of the Chechens in 1864, the most important fighting took place in Dagestan.

In 1860 the Dagestan region was established by the Russian government. From 1865 to 1868 the liberation of serfs and slaves had come to the Caucasus. Economic reform was not far behind. Although the reform was not comprehensive, such developments helped to spur commercial and industrial modernization in Dagestan. The construction of the railroad connecting Dagestan with the rest of Russia brought even greater changes. Various industrial enterprises continued to be built in the late 19th century, including oil refineries and food-processing centers. Huge farms were established in the flatlands and the foothills by Russian landlords and worked by the many Russian peasants who were urged to emigrate to the region. Naturally Russians also brought their cultural practices with them. Many Russian intellectuals

IMAM SHAMIL

Shamil, a leader of the Dagestani and Chechen mountaineers, was born in the *aoul*, or village, Ghumri in Dagestan in 1797. He was elected the third imam in 1834, after the murder of the second imam, Hamza Bey. At the time, the Russian forces were distracted in the western part of the northern Caucasus where they were fighting the Circassians. Shamil took advantage of the situation and was able to extend his influence over the tribes that had not made their loyalties known. Shamil's imamate grew to a considerable size and included parts of western Dagestan, part of Chechnya, and parts of Azerbaijan and Georgia. Under Shamil's guidance, the imamate became stronger and better organized. When the Russians were again prepared to strike against the imamate, he was ready. The Russians met with not only Shamil's formidable forces but also the extremely difficult terrain of the region. The Russians were vulnerable to attack at any moment. The Russian expedition of 1839 almost had to abandon its campaign.

A year earlier, in 1838, the Russians were able to capture the *aoul* Akhoulgo, where Shamil was quartered with his people. But Shamil had escaped. He seemed to have been on the edge of defeat, but Circassians in the west reorganized and resumed their attacks on the Russian fortresses. This diversion gave Shamil time to regroup. The success of the Circassians in seizing a couple of Russian forts and military posts in the western Caucasus rekindled the rebellious spirit of the tribes living in the north-central Caucasus that had previously given up the fight. Shamil got the much-needed support of the Chechens. He then started harassing the Russian troops, often raiding several of their posts in a single day. At the time, in the 1840s, Shamil enjoyed the widespread support of the population, who supplied him with men and horses. Shamil had at his disposal 25,000 cavalrymen. He also introduced rudimentary postal and taxation systems in the territory of his imamate.

In 1843 Shamil captured all of the Russian military posts in Avaria and blockaded the rest of the Russian forces that remained in Dagestan. An accomplished military strategist, he knew when to attack and when to wait until the Russians were exhausted and weakened by disease, cold weather, and the loss of men. He tried to forge an alliance with the Turks and the British during the Crimean War of 1853–56, but neither group would side with him. Due to his increased visibility in the region, he had been widely known and admired in western Europe for his military genius and bravery.

But eventually the Russian army prevailed. In 1857 a large, well-equipped Russian army started closing in on him. In the face of such pressure, many tribes and villages surrendered. Finally, in 1859, isolated with his small group of followers, he surrendered himself and was brought to Saint Petersburg. Later he was exiled to Kaluga, an old town to the south of Moscow, where he was given a mansion and a pension by the czar. One of his sons eventually served in the Russian army. In 1870 he was given permission to go on a pilgrimage to Mecca. He died a year later, in 1871, and was buried in Medina.

and academics set to work studying Dagestani geography, soils, climate, history, languages, and anthropology.

All of this activity gradually led to the emergence of Dagestan's own intelligentsia, who played a considerable role in the pre- and post-revolutionary turmoil that gripped the northern Caucasus. Immediately after the Revolution of 1917 in Russia, when the czar was deposed, Dagestan's intelligentsia, including the mullahs, or Muslim leaders, began to call for an independent Dagestan. They established the society Jamia al Islamia in April 1917, and in September of that year the Dagestani mille-committee.

THE SOVIET PERIOD

After the Russian Revolution, chaos ruled in the entire Caucasus region, including Dagestan. The situation was made all the worse when civil war erupted in Russia. By the early 1920s, the situation began to stabilize. In January 1921 the Soviet government in Moscow established the Dagestan Autonomous Soviet Socialist Republic in the framework of the Russian Soviet socialist republics.

Then in December of that year the Constituent Assembly of Dagestan adopted a constitution and governmental institutions based on the Soviet model. In those years (1921–91) the newly created political entity had a parliament called the Supreme Soviet of the Dagestan Autonomous Soviet Socialist Republic. In the 1980s this parliament had 210 deputies, 82 of whom were women. Although this parliament did not actually wield any power, the fact that more than a third of the deputies were women, as well as the pronounced presence of women in the professional and skilled workforce, opened up opportunities to a group previously denied chances of acquiring greater economic and political power.

HISTORY

Despite the heavy hand of Moscow in the governing of the Caucasus, during the Soviet period Dagestan made a huge leap in economic and social development. A modern oil industry, dozens of large- and middle-sized enterprises in a range of industries, and around 150 electric power plants were established. A more skilled workforce emerged during the period in which agriculture became a more highly industrialized venture.

During World War II, the German army occupied some territory in the northern Caucasus but was stopped by the Soviet army at the Mosdok-Vladikavkas line. Thus, Dagestan was spared occupation by the Germans, but that enemy faction had advanced to within less than 100 miles (161 km)

Chechen refugees gather at a temporary camp in the Dagestani town of Kizlyar, after a raid on their village by Russian troops in June 2005. The event added even more political tension to the already unstable regions of Dagestan and Chechnya.

from the republic's border. During the war several indigenous peoples of the Caucasus, including Dagestan's neighboring groups the Chechens and the Ingush, were deported to central Asia. Again, Dagestani peoples were spared such an atrocity, but the upheaval sent shock waves through the entire Caucasus region. The forced exile served as a powerful reminder of the czarist wars against the native residents of the area.

THE POST-SOVIET PERIOD

The beginning of the 1990s was another period of chaos in the northern Caucasus, including Dagestan. First, every autonomous republic wanted to become an independent, sovereign nation. Then there was a movement for the creation of a mountain republic, which would unite all the ethnic republics of the northern Caucasus. This development was followed by the war in Chechnya, which started in 1994.

In 1996 a cease-fire between Russia and the Chechen rebels was signed in the Dagestani town of Khasavyurt. But in August 1999 Chechen rebels invaded Dagestan with the intention of creating an Islamic republic. The rebels hoped to set off a conflict that would eventually ignite all of the northern Caucasus, much like the Murids had done in the 1830s. This insurgence started the so-called Second Chechen War. Its reverberations are still felt in the northern Caucasus.

The present situation in Dagestan, with the constant incursions of the Chechens, the rampant corruption that affects the government and the economy, the ongoing poverty, and the infighting among different ethnic groups and clans, is unstable. This state of affairs ultimately results in greater controls being instituted by the Russian federal government. Still, the people of Dagestan are working hard to continue building their state and to try and achieve stability and increased prosperity.

GOVERNMENT

SINCE ITS ANNEXATION by Russia in the 19th century, Dagestan has been considered a province in the sprawling Russian empire. In 1921 it became an autonomous republic and part of the Russian Soviet Federated Socialist Republic. Then in 1991, a few months before the Union of Soviet Socialist Republics (USSR) dissolved, the parliament of Dagestan declared the nation independent and christened it with its current name, the Republic of Dagestan. Its capital is Makhachkala.

The following year, on March 31, with other newly independent former Soviet republics, Dagestan signed the treaty that created the Russian Federation. With this historic act, Dagestan again became part of Russia.

"CONSTITUENT SUBJECTS"

Dagestan's borders have shifted slightly several times since the czarist period. But despite the changes in its official boundaries or its official name, very little has changed concerning the country's political life. It was and still is a part of Russia. Even though there are 14 other languages recognized by the state, Dagestan's official language is Russian.

To be more specific, Dagestan is one of Russia's 89 provinces that are called "constituent subjects of the federation." They are grouped, in turn, into seven large federal districts. Dagestan is in the South Federal District, which is composed of political divisions of the northern Caucasus, such as Chechnya and Kabardino-Balkariya.

That means that Dagestan, as with any other member of the federation, is under the control of the federal authorities. The districts were created in 2000 partially to give officials in Moscow more control over the various republics. The system of federal districts also helped establish order and

Opposite: **A policeman guards a law office in the Dagestani town of Kizlyar.**

a central authority for a realm that had partially lapsed into chaos after the USSR broke up.

At the helm of the federal district is a presidential representative who is appointed—without the approval of the Federal Assembly—by the president of Russia. A presidential representative has great political and economic influence in the district and great authority over how regional governments are run.

Many of Russia's constituent subjects, including Dagestan, are still developing their economies and rely on the federal government for money and assistance. Dagestan's 2004 budget came to roughly $581 million.

Russian president Vladimir Putin *(right)* **meets Dagestan's State Council chairman, Magomedali Magomedov, at the Kremlin in Moscow, Russia, in 2003.**

About 83 percent of this money came from the Russian federal budget. Most of the remaining portion came from taxes within Dagestan and the republic's sale of land and small enterprises. As with many states, the money is not enough to sustain the republic through the year. The budget deficit in Dagestan in recent years has been as high as 25 percent.

A UNIQUE REPUBLIC

Some 36 ethnic groups reside in the republic. Due to this complex and diverse range of peoples, the political structure in Dagestan is unique to the Russian Federation. To maintain fairness and order, and a sense of equality among the groups, the government institutions were formed to reflect the percentage of the population each faction represents. This plan was adopted to avoid rivalry and conflict among ethnic groups.

Still, it does not always work smoothly, and the republic's constitution has been amended, or changed, twice since its initial adoption in 1994 in an effort to satisfy and include all of the republic's citizens. A new constitution was adopted in 2003 but is not yet in effect. The system is far from perfect, and the fear of violence and small-scale war consistently grips many of Dagestan's residents. Some Dagestanis even express a nostalgia for the bygone Soviet era, yearning for a strong leader who would be chosen and fully supported by Moscow.

Many critics feel that the presence of a strong leader from outside the region will help to reduce conflict and maintain peace. Some insiders claim that Joseph Stalin, the Soviet leader from the mid-1920s to 1953, is adored in Dagestan, more so than anywhere else in the former Soviet Union, including Georgia. Recent efforts by Russian president Vladimir Putin to strengthen control over the various members of the Russian Federation have been applauded by many Dagestanis.

SYSTEM OF GOVERNMENT

Like the other republics that are members of the federation, Dagestan's system of government mirrors the structure of the national system. Dagestan's constitution set up a parliament, called the People's Assembly, which is composed of one house or chamber. The executive branch is made up of the State Council of the Republic, the Security Council, and the cabinet. As a constituent subject of the Russian Federation, Dagestan sends its own representatives to the Federal Assembly's two chambers, the State Duma (the lower house) and the Federation Council (the upper house).

Dagestan also has a judicial branch, which consists of the Constitutional Court, courts of general jurisdiction (of which the Supreme Court is at the helm), and arbitration courts, which deal with business matters. The Superior Arbitration Court is the top-ranking body in the arbitration-courts system. All judges are appointed for life by authorities in Moscow, a practice many resent, but that others view as politically prudent given the regional and ethnic interests that often divide the republic.

The wide-ranging ethnic makeup of the people of Dagestan has a great effect on the way the republic is governed. The People's Assembly is made up of 72 members, who are elected to four-year terms. The seats are divided up so that the 14 most populous ethnic groups are represented according to the relative size of their populations. In addition, the Constitutional Assembly was created. It is made up of the 121 members of the People's Assembly along with 121 members representing municipal and local councils. The Constitutional Assembly chooses the 14-member State Council. One person is selected from each of Dagestan's most populous ethnic groups. The State Council elects a council chairperson from among its members.

Policemen stand guard on the outskirts of Kizlyar in anticipation of attacks by Chechen militants.

The chairperson of the State Council appoints the cabinet, which is made up of several ministries, including internal affairs; education; health; environment and mineral resources; culture; nationalities and external relations; civil defense emergencies and disaster resources; industry, transportation, and communications; agriculture; social welfare; construction, housing, and communal services; labor and employment; finance; justice; and economy. Three additional organizations, while not official cabinet bureaus, have ministerial status: the board of customs, the taxation police department, and the federal security department.

SYSTEM CHANGES

Dagestan's constitution and political structure have been altered in various ways since independence. When the constitution was amended in March 1998, the People's Assembly voted to change Article 93, which forbade the election of a State Council chairperson from the same ethnic group for two continuous terms. The new wording does not mention or place

Gadzhi Makhachev, who represents Dagestan in the Russian State Duma, speaks on the Chechnya conflict at the Council of Europe in Strasbourg, France.

restrictions based on the individual's ethnicity, but simply states that the chairperson cannot be elected for more than two terms. The change was made in the face of strong pressure from Magomedali Magomedov, chairman of the State Council, who initiated another amendment in 1996 that added two additional years to his first term in office.

These changes provoked strong reactions from opponents as well as the people of Makhachkala, the seat of Dagestan's government. Protestors rallied, claiming that the changes to the constitution created the possibility that the representatives of any given ethnic group could amass a disproportionate amount of power, which they could then use to their own advantage. Such a possibility would be dangerous to Dagestan's unity and weaken the foundations that were formed during centuries of struggle, growth, and compromise.

The issue of balanced and equal representation in government is far from resolved, and new changes are expected. A federal law that was adopted in December 2004 decrees that not only can governors (or presidents) of the republics that make up the Russian Federation be dismissed by the Russian president but that also, beginning in 2005, all governors (or the presidents of the republics) are to be appointed by the Russian president and confirmed by the local legislature. In addition, in his decree of late December 2004, Russian president Vladimir Putin laid out his new plan for appointing governors and informally asked the individual republic's leaders, even those elected just a month prior, to submit their resignation. Most of these original leaders were reappointed to the same posts, but it marked yet another change in the way the region and federation are governed.

ADMINISTRATIVE DIVISIONS

Administratively, Dagestan is divided into 41 districts and one area. In addition, there are 10 cities under the republic's jurisdiction. Among the cities, the largest is Makhachkala, with a population of about 330,000. It was founded by the Russians in 1844 and was called at the time Petrovskaya fortress. Later, after 1857, it was referred to as Petrovsk Port or sometimes Petro-port. From 1921 it was renamed for the famed Dagestani revolutionary of the time, Makhach. It gained in prominence in the early 20th century when the industrial development of Dagestan gained force. Today it is one of the biggest ports on the Caspian Sea, connecting central Asia with southern Ukraine and the rest of mainland Europe via ferries, railroads, and highways.

Other prominent centers among the 10 cities under the republic's jurisdiction are Derbent, founded as a fortress on the caravan route from Asia to Europe; Khasavyurt, where the Russians and Chechens signed a cease-fire in 1996; and Kizlyar, where Salman Raduyev, a Chechen rebel, held hostages during the conflict.

ECONOMY

LIKE ANY COUNTRY that has been undergoing a radical political and social transformation, Dagestan has struggled to place its economy on solid footing. The war and conflicts that still grip neighboring Chechnya and often spill into Dagestani territory only add to the instability.

The republic's legacy has also added to the difficulties in strengthening its industrial and economic base. At one time, Dagestan's economy existed to support and bolster the Soviet empire. During the years of Soviet domination, all commercial enterprises in the various republics were closely interconnected.

With the fall of the Soviet Union, these close ties were broken, and it became immediately evident how weak Dagestan's economy was. Not only did businesses collapse, due to the lack of Soviet support on which many industries had grown to depend, but many goods needed by consumers and business owners alike became unavailable or in short supply.

Until around the period from 1996 to 1997, Dagestan's economy showed little sign of recovery from the sudden collapse of the Soviet Union. Then, as the Russian economy started to improve, Dagestan's followed suit. But the upturn did not last long.

In the summer of 1998, Russia experienced another financial crisis. The Russian currency, the ruble, was devalued. Although that ruined some businesses—export firms in particular—and claimed many people's savings, it also helped small- and medium-sized enterprises in agriculture and the food-processing industry to develop.

These are two spheres of the economy in which many Dagestanis find work. In 1998, of all the companies and business ventures in operation in Dagestan, 48 percent were somehow related to farming and the processing and manufacturing of food.

Opposite: **Dagestani vendors unload fresh produce at a market. Fruit cultivated in the republic's orchards is sold not only at local markets but also in other parts of Russia.**

A potato field at a farm in the Tsumada district.

AGRICULTURE

Agriculture accounts for about 35 percent of Dagestan's annual earnings. A widespread industry, workers and officials are trying to make farming ventures more productive and efficient. Animal husbandry makes up about 65 percent of all agricultural activities in Dagestan. Sheep breeding remains the main focus, especially for mountain residents for whom herding has been the main source of income for generations. Still, cattle breeding has gained in importance, and there are a few pig farms.

Planting and harvesting have always been challenging for Dagestan's agricultural workers. Due to poor, often infertile land, native residents often had to trade or barter goods to obtain grain. In the past they bargained with Russian and other merchants, as well as with the cossacks living in the lowlands of northern Dagestan. These activities still go on today. They are crucial exchanges that have become standard for the Dagestanis living in the mountains and on the lowlands. Currently there are only 0.75 acres (0.3 hectares) of arable land per capita in Dagestan.

The irrigated lowlands are fertile and produce a variety of crops, including winter wheat, corn, sunflowers, potatoes, melons, and grapes. Still, only about 15 percent of Dagestan's land can be cultivated. Because of this lack of arable land, priority is given to growing vegetables and fruit, especially grapes. Orchards of peach, apricot, plum, cherry, and other fruits cover about 75,000 acres (30,000 hectares). The fruit is sold not only in local markets but throughout Russia. These ventures thus contribute considerably to the Dagestani economy.

Wine making is one of the traditional occupations of Dagestanis. It was and still is an important branch of the economy. Dagestanis even make a type of brandy that was highly prized in the days of the Soviet Union. The brandy comes from a Derbent distillery that is 150 years old. Before the political and economic reforms known as perestroika (meaning "rebuilding" or "restructuring") were instituted in the USSR, about 45 percent of all the grapes harvested in Russia were grown in Dagestan. Today the wine-making industry has experienced a downturn. The total amount of grapes harvested annually has dropped five times from its peak level in 1985 before the onset of perestroika. But, after many years, Dagestan and the Russian federal government, with the governments of other wine-producing regions, have begun to make greater efforts in developing this aspect of the nation's economy. Dagestani growers and winemakers are hoping that, someday soon, the nation's wine industry will achieve its former glory.

Dagestan is also graced with numerous bodies of water and a wealth of aquatic life. In the Caspian Sea and in the river deltas and lakes, there are valuable reserves of fish, including sturgeon, salmon, herring, and trout. Fish processing used to be one of the most important industries in Dagestan. But overfishing substantially reduced the size of the catches and, consequently, this industry has lost importance.

INDUSTRY AND CONSTRUCTION

Industry in Dagestan is quite diverse and includes aspects of oil and gas ventures, chemical manufacturing, construction, the production of machinery and tools, glassmaking, transportation and communications, textile manufacturing, fishing, food processing, and wine making. The main industrial facilities are concentrated in the republic's largest cities, mostly in the capital Makhachkala, which is also one of the biggest ports on the Caspian Sea. The republic's second-largest city, Derbent, and a few of the other major urban centers—Buynaksk, Kizlyar, Kaspiysk, Khasavyurt, Izberbash, and Kizilyurt—support their own significant manufacturing and industrial base. These important economic centers, with the exception of Buynaksk, are connected by the main railroad and highway. Food-processing enterprises are scattered throughout Dagestan and are commonly found near large farms, vineyards, and ports.

In the last decade, the economy has shifted its focus significantly. For example, before the early 1990s, the manufacturing of machinery and the food-processing industry accounted for almost 80 percent of the republic's industrial output. Now, that figure has shrunk to 44 percent. Meanwhile, the energy sector's contribution rose from 5 to 45 percent. Dagestan, like the entire region surrounding the Caspian Sea, has some oil and gas deposits. Their existence has been known since ancient times, due to natural leaks bringing the resources to the surface. Not until 1924 did exploratory drilling, initiated by the Soviets, begin in earnest. They started to extract oil on a commercial basis in 1936. Up to the end of the 1950s, the main sites were in southern Dagestan but, starting in 1958, the center of the industry moved to the Nogay Steppe in northern Dagestan. At present, the oil industry is concentrated in the northern Dagestani town of Yuzhno-Sukhokumsk and in central Dagestan in Izberbash and

Apartment blocks in Makhachkala. The increasing demand for urban housing contributes significantly to recent growth in the republic's construction industry.

Achisu. The oil, besides being used and refined in Dagestan, is transported to other regions of Russia as well as abroad. According to official data, Dagestan now produces around 310,000 tons, or about 2 million barrels, of oil and 25,250 million cubic feet (715 million cubic m) of gas per year. Exports of oil and gas constitute more than half of the republic's hard currency proceeds. Production and extraction levels have continued to rise as the oil is of better quality than that found in the Ural region of Russia. But continued investments and development are necessary. Local resources are limited, and luring foreign investors has proved difficult due to the political and economic instability of the region.

The oil is exported via a pipeline that crosses Dagestan from Baku, Azerbaijan, to Makhachkala via Grozny, Chechnya. It is then sent on to the port of Novorossiysk (in Krasnodar) on the Black Sea. Next, ships transport it via the Bosporus in Turkey to markets in Europe. Since the war in Chechnya has often disrupted the flow of this pipeline, the Russians have built another branch from Makhachkala to just north of the Chechen border, thus bypassing the dangerous zone. Today, oil and gas pipelines crossing Dagestan measure a total of 329 miles (530 km) in length.

ELECTRIC POWER

Dagestan has about 30 percent of the hydroelectric power resources of the northern Caucasus, and it has the potential to generate more. Dagestan's hydroelectric power stations produce 2.76 million kilowatt hours (kWh) but are capable of generating almost twice that amount.

Strides are being made to strengthen this aspect of the economy. Several new hydroelectric power plants are to be built along the Sulak River. Many in the region have already been in operation since the middle of the 20th century. The most powerful is the Chirkeiskaya hydroelectric power plant, capable of generating 1 million kWh. It was built in the 1970s on the Sulak River at Chirkey. Two other plants have been completed on the same river—at Chiryurt and Kizilyurt.

Large plants are also found on the Karakoysu River at Gergebil as well as along the Terek River at Kagarlinsk. The plant at Irganay, able to produce more than 0.8 million kWh, has also been completed. In addition, there are as many as 100 small hydroelectric operations located near various villages. Dagestan's power plants are able to satisfy the region's energy needs. The republic is also connected via power lines to the rest of Russia and is able to export some energy to other parts of the federation.

The vast infrastructure of Dagestan's oil industry—including its oil-extraction facilities, pipelines, and power plants—was built during the Soviet period, mostly from the 1950s through the 1970s, long before the recent pressures to further develop the energy sector. One positive legacy of this Soviet development has been that the republic retains an extensive force of experienced engineers and technical personnel, educated and skilled in the technicalities of the energy industry. Despite the presence of this trained workforce, Dagestan's oil industry, after the economic challenges of the late 1980s and early 1990s, requires much-needed updating and improvement to maximize its potential. Only through renovation and the development of additional reserves will Dagestan continue to benefit from its valuable underground resources.

TRANSPORTATION AND COMMUNICATIONS

Geographically, Dagestan is well situated, connecting Russia with the rest of Asia via the Caspian Sea. For centuries, an important trade route wound through the region. The city of Derbent was built along this route to protect the merchants who used it.

Dagestanis set up make-shift stalls beside their vehicles at the Saturday market in Agvali.

А station guard patrols the platform before a train that is part of the Trans-Siberian Railroad departs. To get to other parts of Russia, most Dagestanis find rail travel a more economical alternative to flying.

Today, the republic's transportation infrastructure is much more extensive. Dagestan is connected to the rest of Russia, as well as to Azerbaijan and Georgia, by railroads, airports, and highways, some of which were built in the late 1800s. A main railroad line stretches from Baku to Astrakhan via Derbent and Makhachkala. The route then splits, with one branch heading north along the Volga River and the other winding its way to Kazakhstan. A different branch goes from Makhachkala to Gudermes, near the Chechen capital of Grozny, through Stavropol and then via Rostov-on-Don to Moscow and to Kharkov in the Ukraine. Altogether there are about 290 miles (465 km) of railway in the country. So, despite its rugged and often inhospitable terrain, Dagestan suffers from no lack of connection to the world beyond its borders.

Roads total more than 5,280 miles (8,500 km), but at least half of them are unpaved. These simple byways are understandable in the mountain regions where the small population, lack of industrial centers, and difficult terrain prevent the need for a major or highly developed system of highways, which would also be costly to maintain. In total, there are around 190 miles (300 km) of major highway in the republic. There is a thoroughfare from Moscow to Baku, built long ago, that crosses into Dagestan. Other important roads are located along the Caspian shoreline as well as between Makhachkala, Grozny, and Stavropol.

A significant port on the Caspian Sea, Makhachkala draws merchant and fishing fleets and is the site of a major terminal for transporting oil from sea to land. Plans to reconstruct the port, which links with the rail system, have been stalled due to lack of investment. Makhachkala also has a major airport, 9 miles (15 km) from the city. The capital's developed infrastructure has made Dagestan a major transportation and communications hub in the northern Caucasus and Caspian Sea region.

HANDICRAFTS

Traditional handicrafts are a significant, though minor, part of Dagestan's economy. Since ancient times, the people of Dagestan have been known for their handicrafts. Many villages specialized in a certain trade and became known by it. Some communities were famous for their sheepskins or for their tools made of steel, iron, or copper. Others were well known for their rugs. Some villages developed expertise in fashioning jewelry or sabers and other weapons, while some enclaves produced pottery.

The industrialization of the economy resulted in handicrafts and folk practices dying out. Still, many traditional crafts persist in Dagestan, as the country's ethnic groups contribute their artistic styles and types of handicrafts. The handicrafts of Dagestan are a rich legacy that serves not only as a connection to the past but also as a means of honoring and extending the traditions to future generations. While in the past many handicrafts resulted in the creation of something practical and useful in the family's everyday life, today many of these objects have taken on the status of art. For example, the Lezgin and Tabasaran peoples make rugs that are highly prized, while the villages of Kubachi and Gotsatl are famous for their distinctive, glittering pieces of jewelry.

DEVELOPMENT PLANS

In late 1997, when the Russian economy first showed signs of significant improvement, the government of Dagestan adopted a program of social and economic development. A number of laws supporting the plan were drafted at the time as well.

The regional program that emerged sought to boost the economy by using existing production facilities, resources, and skilled personnel with only a minimum of external financing. Top priorities included the further development of the infrastructure with a specific focus on small- and medium-sized enterprises that produced consumer goods and provided services. A number of critical projects aimed at stimulating business in Dagestan were started under this program, but the Russian financial crisis of August 1998 and the 1999 invasion of Dagestan by the Chechens—with the subsequent Russian military intervention—has stalled the progress of this revitalization effort.

A similar program was adopted in the fall of 2004. It stressed the need to create new jobs and increase income levels. By official count 1.366 million Dagestanis—65 percent of the population—had an income below the poverty line. Alleviating poverty has become an overriding concern. Government officials who are advocating the change call for reducing unemployment and increasing wages. Thus, it is necessary to further develop businesses of all sizes, especially in the energy sector, to bolster transportation systems, including oil and gas pipelines, and above all to adopt legislation that would promote and encourage increased investment. According to recent figures, Dagestan would need $4 billion and until 2010 to implement this program. Only 19.3 percent of that money would come from the federal budget; 15.2 percent would come from the republic's budget, 1.8 percent from municipal budgets, and 63.3 percent from private investments and loans.

The main obstacle to implementing this program, especially from the perspective of private investors, is the extremely volatile political and social climate, due not only to the war in Chechnya, but also to old clan rivalries and to general lawlessness and corruption. Black-market operations and some businesses' failure to report revenue are among the factors that are impeding economic growth and stability. By some private economists' estimates, the black market was responsible for approximately 70 percent of the gross domestic product (GDP) during the 1990s. From 1996 to 1997 that figure reached 76 percent. In some industries, such as food processing or the production of building materials, it has been as high as 80 percent, and in the vodka-distillation industry, it has been as high as 95 percent. In 1997, out of 2,494 registered enterprises, only 778 had been reporting and paying taxes.

ENVIRONMENT

THE RAPID INDUSTRIALIZATION of Dagestan and the northern Caucasus region in the 20th century led to the pollution of many valuable resources, most notably the Caspian Sea. More efficient and well-planned scientific approaches to agriculture and water management are needed as Dagestanis are slowly realizing the need to protect their valuable natural resources for the future.

DAMAGE TO THE SEA

Pollutants are discharged directly into the Caspian Sea or through the municipal water collection and treatment systems that are often so obsolete they are unable to filter out a majority of the pollutants. Through the years toxins slowly reached levels that are dangerous not only to the many aquatic

Left: **A view of the Caspian Sea from the city of Derbent.**

Opposite: **Rocks on a beach along the Caspian shore near Derbent.**

species living in the sea but also to the people living along or near its shores. Dagestan's water collection and treatment systems are in desperate need of investment capital for improvements. Years of neglect and inattention to the problems have only made them worse. In addition, the creation of new environmentally sensitive factories and facilities is a costly proposition, one the Dagestani government and business community are unprepared to face.

DAMAGE TO THE LAND

The republic's valuable land and soil resources have not escaped the harmful influence of industry either. Chemical plants, oil-extraction facilities, and coastal fish-processing operations account for a large portion of the environmental damage. The many hydroelectric power plants built along the rivers have damaged biological resources in the interior as well, although to a lesser extent. Reducing industrial pollution is a top priority in Dagestan's, and Russia's, attempts to improve the environment.

But there are other urgent problems as well. In some areas, particularly in the Nogay Steppe, where abundant water reserves are lacking, erosion and desertification have radically transformed the face of the land. The salinization, or increased salt content, of the soil is another grave development. The land bears the stress of a fast-growing human and livestock population as well as the increased cultivation of more and more acreage. Short-term solutions instituted in the first decades of the 20th century initially eased the impact and damage but ultimately only added to the salt levels in the soil. In a vicious cycle, this process has led to even more extensive desertification in some areas.

Wars, most recently with Chechen militants, have also been a major cause of environmental degradation in Dagestan. The use of military weapons has scarred and poisoned the land, and the cost of cleaning up afterward, even if the land never completely recovers, is immense.

Opposite: **Poor or outdated drainage systems are an all too common sight in some parts of Dagestan.**

Below: **A woman shakes a rug clean outside her destroyed home in the Dagestani village of Novolakhskoye, after Russian forces crushed a Chechen incursion.**

DAGESTANIS

ABOUT 36 ETHNIC GROUPS live in the republic, whose total population is approximately 2.1 million. These ethnic groups are loosely distributed among three major divisions: Caucasian, Turkic, and Slavic. Most of the groups are native to the area, while others immigrated to the region and have lived there for generations.

The mountains that dominate southern Dagestan are home to a wide variety of tribes that have thrived in the region. Some of these tribal groupings are small, consisting of between 1,000 and 2,000 members. Adding to this diversity are the peoples and ethnic groups that live in the lowlands and the cities. Most Dagestanis are Muslim, but a portion is made up of Russians, Ukrainians, and other primarily Christian nationalities. A small Jewish population is also present.

Left: **Avar men gather in a town square. Avars make up the largest ethnic group in the republic.**

Opposite: **A Dagestani woman plies her wares, richly patterned carpets, in the coastal city of Derbent.**

A Dargin woman surveys the scene from her window. The Dargins are the largest minority group in Dagestan.

ETHNIC-LINGUISTIC GROUPS

The nation's largest ethnic group is the Avars. They represent about 25 percent of the entire population of Dagestan. They live mainly in the mountainous and hilly regions of western Dagestan and northern Azerbaijan. They are followed by Dargins, who make up about 15 percent of the populace, Kumyks (about 12 percent), Lezgins and Russians (about 11 percent each), Laks (about 5 percent), and Tabasarans and Azeris (about 4 percent each).

All of the peoples living in Dagestan are culturally similar, since most of them have interacted with one another for centuries. They also practice the same religion—Islam. According to the languages these various peoples speak, they can be divided into three main groups: Dagestanis, Turkic peoples, and Slavs.

The Caucasian people speak Dagestan tongues, which are a branch of the Ibero-Caucasian family of languages. The same or a similar branch is spoken by other peoples living in the Caucasus, mostly in the northern districts of Azerbaijan and in some villages of Georgia, as well as in the republics of Chechnya and Ingushetiya. The Dagestan tongues themselves are subdivided into several related languages. For example, the Avars speak one form of a

An elderly man, wearing a traditional hat, rests on a bench outside his home.

Dagestan tongue, while the Lezgins and Dargins each speak their own form.

The Turkic and Iranian language groups are also represented in the country. The Nogay peoples are Turkic groups that came to the northern Caucasus in the 13th century. They now live near Dagestan in the Stavropol, Chechnya, and Karachaevo-Cherkessia regions. The language of the Mountain Jews reflects Iranian origins.

The Slavs speak Slavic tongues, mostly Russian and Ukrainian, while most Dagestanis are bilingual, using Russian in their everyday life. One notable exception are the residents of remote mountain villages, who have little exposure to or use for Russian in their day-to-day existence. About half of the present population, mostly the people who make up the mountainous tribes, is indigenous to the areas where they have lived for thousands of years.

Clearly, Dagestan is a land where several vibrant and diverse cultures intersect. While ethnic strife, intertribal rivalries, and clashes between clans and factions have divided the region, Dagestanis have, for the most part, been able to live peaceably side by side for centuries.

LIFESTYLE

HUNDREDS OF YEARS of living in close proximity has contributed to the merging and blending of the customs and lifeways of Dagestan's many cultural and ethnic groups. The mountainous terrain and the residents' constant resistance to invasions have shaped the lifestyle and character of the Dagestani people. Social and political changes have influenced their lifestyles as well. During the Soviet era, all non-Russian cultures were affected by the empire's dominance. This had both positive and negative consequences.

Modern Dagestan is a complex mix of the old and the new. People's lifestyles often depend on the wide variance in income. The gap between city and village life is striking, as it is in many other parts of the Russian Federation, and this gulf grows only wider year by year. Most women work outside the home while at the same time shouldering the main responsibility for household chores.

Traditions are honored and respected, particularly in rural areas, where most of the populace lives. As a result, ancestral mores and ways have powerfully influenced Dagestani culture as a whole. To this day, respect for the older generations and the past is a keystone of the culture. Despite the nation's long and turbulent history, many of the customs and traditions of Dagestan have survived for hundreds and thousands of years. While Russian culture and lifestyles have grown increasingly more universally similar throughout the Russian Federation, many of Dagestan's indigenous peoples have worked hard to maintain their own unique traditions and cultural identity.

Above: **A man guides his donkey along a rural road.**

Opposite: **Traditional homes in Kubachi.**

Opposite: **An Avar father and daughter.**

NAMUS

Namus (nah-MOOS), meaning "support" or "the ability to give," lies at the heart of the unwritten moral code of the Dagestani people. A person with *namus* is generous, reliable, affable, compassionate, and conscientious. For any Dagestani, *namus* is an ideal to pursue and a concept that forms the cornerstone of family and community life.

IMMEDIATE FAMILY

The typical Dagestani family is a nuclear grouping, consisting of a married couple and their offspring. Rural dwellers tend to have larger families than people living in the city, for whom two children tends to be the average. In cities and villages alike, though, boys enjoy a higher status than girls. Dagestani society is highly patriarchal—lineage is traced through the father's side. Traditionally, the father and husband is the head of the family. He is responsible for the well-being of family members and also for managing all their property and assets. Although both men and women typically work, it is the men who must ensure financial security for the family. Thus, not surprisingly, they typically have the final say in decision making within the family. Only rarely does a woman become the head of a family. This does, however, happen in special circumstances, such as when the male head of the household dies or moves abroad in search of work. In such cases, the oldest woman then assumes responsibility for the family's well-being.

More often than not, particularly in rural areas, young people live with their parents until they marry. After marriage, young men try to settle as close as possible to their parents' home. Grandparents maintain close contact with their children and grandchildren, helping the new families with household chores and with the upbringing of children. Occasionally, elderly parents move in with their children, typically with their son's family, thus enabling the young to take better care of the old. Small children, as soon as they are able, are expected to help their grandparents.

Polygamy, or multiple marriages, has a long history in Dagestan. Traditionally, both Islam and Judaism permitted the practice. Among Jews, rabbis and wealthy men typically had two wives when the first wife was unable to bear children. Muslim men could have up to four wives. Although forbidden by law, polygamy among Muslims still exists in Dagestan, mainly in rural areas. Often, having little influence on their husbands' decisions and fearing abandonment, women in multiple marriages submit to their spouse's behavior and guidance, be it good or bad.

EXTENDED FAMILY

Several families from the paternal side form a *tuhum*, or clan. The size of a *tuhum* depends on the ethnic group. Some *tuhums* are made up of as few as five families; others consist of as many as 70. In keeping with Dagestani society's patriarchal nature, a *tuhum* is rarely headed by a woman. Instead, it is typically headed by an authoritative man, selected on the basis of

his personal qualities and experience and the role he plays in the life of the community. In some ethnic groups, the oldest male is chosen as the head of the *tuhum*.

Within the clan, the care and protection of relatives are among the most sacred duties. Clan obligations include the extended family as well, and members are expected to take care of nieces and nephews, cousins, and even great-aunts and great-uncles. The role of the *tuhum* is particularly significant during major events in a person's life. At such times, members of a *tuhum* support one another financially, contributing when someone builds a house, celebrates a wedding, or organizes a funeral.

The clan assumes responsibility for the behavior and actions of all of its members. The clan takes pride in every member's achievements just as the whole clan is also culpable for his or her misdeeds. The practice promotes unity as the clan shares its members' glories, while shame, as the Dagestanis say, "turns faces black." If a serious problem arises, the head of the family summons a family council, in which the elders have the final word.

COMMUNITY

In the past, poverty and hardship have made it difficult to survive without the support of close community bonds. As a result, people have developed close ties not only within their extended family, but also with their neighbors and the other residents of their village or town.

Any individual or family in a Muslim village can receive assistance from their *jamaat* (jah-mah-AHT), or local rural community. When someone's house is destroyed by fire or a mudslide, for instance, the community provides all possible support, including the financial means to get the victims on sure footing once again. People also help one another by

A clan gathering in Kvanada, Dagestan.

picking crops, shearing sheep, and building houses. Family, friends, and neighbors only need to be asked to help, and they do what is within their means or at their disposal. People are expected to help one another willingly and with pleasure. Even the elderly, who may be unable to contribute physically, encourage and cheer on the workers. After work, everyone enjoys a large festive meal, prepared by the host family.

Dagestani villages still have councils of elders, which consist of the most highly respected members of the community. In the past, these councils, relying on customary and Islamic laws, regulated a wide range of social issues. During the Soviet era, however, the role of these councils in Dagestani village life became significantly weakened.

In cities, community ties are somewhat weaker than in rural areas. However, mutual bonds are still strong in comparison to those in many Western nations or in regions that make up the rest of the Russian Federation. City dwellers in Dagestan keep in close touch with their families, friends, and neighbors, providing one another with the support necessary to successfully navigate their daily lives.

HOSPITALITY

As one popular Dagestani expression states, "Even if a guest comes unexpectedly, he is never unexpected, because we are waiting for a guest always, every day, every hour, and every minute." With such a sentiment, it comes as no surprise that hospitality and the ability to be a welcoming and gracious host are values highly prized in Dagestani society. The best bed, the best food, and the best seats at the table are all reserved for guests. Moreover, if a guest expresses his or her fondness for an object in the house, he or she is typically given it as a present.

In the Caucasus, a special term exists to describe a guest—*kounak* (koo-NAHK). A traveler of any origin and religious background, no matter whether he or she comes from a friendly community or a rival faction, a *kounak* is always received with the highest honor and dignity. He or she is unquestionably offered an overnight stay, food, and personal safety; and the visitor's belongings are always ensured protection. A *kounak* maintains close contacts with the family, and if he stays repeatedly at the same house, he becomes an honorary *kounak*. Such a person then has the opportunity to become even closer than a family member. An honorary *kounak* is invited to the most important family events and participates in making important decisions. Choosing to stay overnight with other people subsequently becomes an insult to the host family. The title of honorary *kounak* is also hereditary, and the *kounak* of the father ranks higher than one's own patriarch.

MOTHERLAND

To say "I swear by this soil" is the most sacred oath a Dagestani can make. The homeland is considered a sacred place. Even if people raised in rural settings move to faraway cities, they preserve the house built by their

Guests enjoy their host's hospitality at a feast in the Lak region of Dagestan.

ancestors, often high in the mountains, and pass it on from generation to generation. Children are brought to the home to see the land of their ancestors and to listen to the stories told about their grandparents by village elders. Before dying, many Dagestanis express a wish to be buried in their home village.

Away from their homeland, Dagestanis attempt to stay in touch with compatriots. Moving to a new place, they form communities where they attempt to preserve the atmosphere of their homeland. As a rule, relations among Dagestanis living abroad tend to be strong. Dagestani expatriates speak the language of their ancestors and preserve Dagestani traditions and customs. In different parts of the world, people of Dagestani origin have been known to change their names to Dagestanly, which stands for Dagestani. Even far away, this abiding unity makes the Dagestani feel accountable to their family and to their entire clan. This feeling of responsibility is often a great incentive to work hard and to achieve prominent positions in society.

A group of schoolboys takes a break from their soccer game.

CHILDREN

Dagestan has the highest birth rate in Russia, and it is rare to see a Dagestani family without children. The birth of the first child is cause for celebration. If it is a boy, a huge feast is held, and guests come to offer their wishes of health and happiness for the newborn and his mother. The birth of a girl, in contrast, is usually celebrated only in the family circle.

Naming a child is a serious matter. Names are believed to influence fate and thus are chosen carefully. Many Dagestanis believe that a name gives spirit, determines the child's future life, and provides lifelong protection. Both health and luck depend on a person's name. Therefore, Dagestanis often name their children after legendary national heroes or deceased family members who enjoyed a long life. Recently, parents have started to give their children the names of their grandparents or highly respected family members who are still alive. The name is announced to a circle of friends and family members who gather in the newborn's house. An esteemed guest takes the baby in his or her hands and pronounces the child's name three times. If the baby is a boy, "Grow up, *dzhigit*! Be like the person whose name you carry!" is proclaimed. In particular, the residents of the village Kubachi have a strong belief in the power of names. If a child was thought to be delicate, parents have been known to change its name in the hope of imbuing the child with a hardier, stronger constitution.

All the milestones in a child's life, including the first tooth, first haircut, and first step, are celebrated. When the baby turns 40 days old, the family cuts the child's hair and nails. The appearance of the first tooth is also cause for blessings and praise. In some parts of Dagestan, a baby's first step is the time when a father tests his child's willpower. If the baby makes the first steps in front of the father, the father gives it a light nudge, so that the child falls to the floor. If the child is able to get up without help, a feast follows. If the child fails to get up, it is sent to the house of friends or relatives. After several days, the child is brought back home, and the ritual is repeated until the child is able to stand up on its own.

Girls and boys are brought up differently, and an extensive network of people takes part in their respective upbringings. A girl usually spends a lot of time with her mother and the other women in the family. She is brought up to be patient and taught that she will be dependent on her husband. From early childhood, a girl performs household chores. In southern Dagestan, where the art of carpet making is especially popular, girls also learn how to make these elegant textiles.

In contrast to girls, boys are brought up to be the future heads of their families. While boys also help their parents, their workload is limited, which leaves them plenty of time for games and sports. Boys start working later in life. Sons of craftsmen start learning the secrets of their father's profession from the age of 12. Still, no matter what the sex of the child is, diligence is the main virtue that parents instill in all of their offspring.

EDUCATION

Dagestan possesses an increasingly more educated and skilled modern workforce. During the Soviet period, Dagestan—like all other regions in the former Soviet Union—achieved near total literacy. Education in Dagestan was modeled after the Soviet system and, at higher levels, was conducted mostly in Russian. This was an immense achievement for a country where, just a few decades earlier, most of the tribes did not even have their own written language. Although some groups used Arabic script to write in their language, the practice was not widespread.

In primary schools, some children were taught in their local language, though students were required to learn in Russian. Since Russian was the official state language of the USSR, it also became the predominant language of instruction in high schools and universities. That status has changed little today, as Russian is Dagestan's unofficial language and continues to be the language of education as well as of politics and everyday life.

In the early 1890s, there were eight primary schools in all of Dagestan (which had a population of about 0.66 million at the time) with a little more than 200 students enrolled. In addition, there were religious schools in village mosques where pupils learned Islamic law under the guidance of a mullah. Religious schools, however, were suppressed during the Soviet era. A hundred years later, by the end of the 1980s and just before the collapse of the USSR, Dagestan had more than 1,500 primary, middle, high, and vocational schools. Enrollment totaled more than half a million pupils. In addition, the republic had four institutions of higher education, including Dagestan State University, and a Pedagogical Institute, now called Pedagogical University. A branch of the USSR Academy of Science, with its four research institutes, was established in Dagestan. In other

words, at that time, the education system reflected and corresponded to the needs of its local industries. Any Dagestani, if he or she wanted or was permitted to, could go to any Soviet educational institution anywhere in the country and compete with any other potential student to gain admittance to that particular institution. Education, even at the university level, was free.

A lot has changed since then. Educational reforms have been attempted. Schools have increasingly charged tuition, and corruption continues to dog the system as it does many other institutions in Dagestan. Today, the entire education system is in need of reform. Some initiatives have been introduced, but slowly and with much resistance from various groups who feel the changes will negatively impact their access to learning. In addition, Muslim extremists have become active in the region. They have been helped by Middle Eastern Islamists, who spent about $1 million between 1992 and 1996 alone to build approximately five madrassas (schools for Islamic instruction), 40 mosques, and to renovate another 16 mosques in

Dagestan's national system of education is slowly being reformed. Although the traditional Soviet model predominates, Muslim ideals and ideology continue to have an increased influence in some schools.

A school celebration on the Day of Knowledge (September 1), when children bring flowers to mark the beginning of a new school year.

Dagestan. Religious education is, in other words, reestablishing itself in the republic. Nonetheless, even in remote villages, Dagestanis receive the best education possible. Despite changes in the economy and in society, Dagestanis remain an informed and educated people.

BEFORE MARRIAGE

Dagestanis have always treated marriage with the utmost seriousness. Traditionally, young people did not leave their parents' home before they were married. A young man chose his future wife from several candidates suggested by his parents. Following his selection, his family named certain high-powered intermediaries to negotiate with the girl's parents. In most ethnic groups, people married inside their clan and, very often, they married their cousins. This was shaped mostly by financial considerations: clans did not want to lose the property they had held for generations. Occasionally, members of different clans intermarried. In general, though, negotiators discussed the size and the form of *kalym*, the dowry or gifts that the groom had to supply the bride's parents to ensure that the girl's needs were met and to cover related expenses. Successful negotiations were followed by an engagement and marriage.

These traditions have gradually begun to change. More and more often, young people find partners of their own choosing, and marrying within one's own ethnic group or clan has become less of a social or economic imperative. Although some people still prefer to subscribe to this once traditional pattern, inter-ethnic marriages are common in the republic's cities. While Dagestani women usually marry men from other Dagestani ethnic groups, Dagestani men more and more often marry Russian, Ukrainian, and Belarusian women.

Cohabitation is uncommon. A couple can opt for a civil nonreligious marriage ceremony, but most choose to have a religious one as well. Unwritten laws guide the financial arrangements of the marriage. To share the costs of the ceremony, parents appoint trustees among close friends and family. As a rule, only happily married couples are asked to help organize a wedding, as this is believed to bring good luck to the young couple. Trustees partially share the expenses. The groom's parents are traditionally responsible for providing the young family with housing, and the family of the bride is responsible for furnishing the interior of the newlyweds' home. Today, young couples often decide where to live on their own.

The attitude toward separation is also changing. Divorce has gained wider acceptance and become more common. Divorce rates are higher in urban areas, because cities have relatively more liberal social norms and a higher ratio of Slavic peoples for whom the practice has lost much of its stigma. Nevertheless, Dagestan still has the lowest divorce rate in Russia and one of the lowest rates in Europe.

WEDDINGS

A Dagestani wedding is a big feast, to which all family members and friends are invited. While city dwellers send bright invitation cards to their friends in the mail, a specially selected person goes from house to house to spread the word in villages.

Weddings are typically celebrated in early fall, between the traditional times when grapes were harvested and then turned into wine. The unions are celebrated when the weather is warm enough for people to stay outside and when fruit and vegetables are in abundance. Food is cooked in large amounts, so that no one leaves the feast hungry. Alcohol consumption is limited, as public drunkenness is perceived as a shameful practice.

At an Islamic religious ceremony, the imam reads a special prayer and tells the young couple: "In joy, in separation or in sorrow, always remember the blessedness of marriage and the first embrace. Forget about the last quarrel." A Christian religious ceremony, held in a church, often has a solemn touch. In front of the altar, the couple swears to be faithful to each other and to love each other until death.

Marriage celebrations usually start simultaneously in the houses of both the bride and the groom. The bride's departure from her parents' house and her arrival at the groom's house are a major part of the festivities. First, the groom's delegation arrives at the bride's house to the accompaniment of songs. Parting with the daughter, the mother gives her advice and wishes her happiness in marriage. Soon, the wedding procession, with family and friends in tow, leaves for the groom's house. If his house is not far away, the festive crowd walks. Carrying torches, family and guests play music and compete in games. Jesters perform funny sketches. The women from the groom's family carry presents and sing, praising the young couple, as well as the bride's father and brothers.

A bridegroom performs a ritual dance at his wedding.

In cities, the wedding procession consists of beautifully decorated cars, and drivers repeatedly honk their horns to attract everyone's attention. The future mother-in-law meets the bride with the following words: "May you bring us happiness and wealth; may you not die before you see your great grandchildren at your knees." To demonstrate their happiness, the groom's family meets the bride with an ancient dance. People throw nuts, grain, candy, and coins at the bride.

"Dear bride and groom," the *tamada* (tah-mah-DAH), the master of the wedding ceremony, says, "it is a very important day. Many guests have gathered here in this room. Now you should thank your parents, the organizers of the wedding. Give them a bow for everything they have done to bring you up. Give them a bow for their blessing!" Guests, especially the couple's parents, often meet these words with tears. The couple then gives their parents a deep bow to express their love, respect, and sense of duty. The celebration extends late into the evening.

Preparing the bed for the couple's first night, women roll a small boy on the newlyweds' bed and ask God to bless the young couple, giving them only boys. The next morning, women bring the bride new clothes and take away her old dress. The bride then prepares breakfast for her new husband and his friends, and the feast goes on for three days.

DAGESTANI MEN

Yag' (YAKH), or masculinity, is a concept that stands at the core of the ethical code of Dagestani men. This notion comprises honor, dignity, courage, fortitude, diligence, honesty, nobility, generosity, respect for the elderly, and kindness to the weak and the poor. *Yag'* also implies patience, tidiness, and duty. A man is not expected to complain about thirst and hunger, cold and heat. He is not allowed to show signs of tiredness when talking to an elder. A man is discouraged from showing

A group of friends shares a meal at the foot of Mount Addala Shukhgelmezr.

his fear. In addition, a man's superior status is unquestioned and does not need to be proved. It is considered innate. His role as the head of the family supports his dominant position. Most Dagestani women, whether devoutly religious or not, respect the man's authority.

A Dagestani boy is brought up according to the principles of *yag'*. Starting in his teen years, he learns the ethical code, socializing in the *godekan* (ghoh-deh-KAHN), the village square. There he also learns to develop reserve, humility, and self-control—qualities highly valued in a land of extreme ethnic diversity and economic hardship.

DAGESTANI WOMEN

The notion of intelligence, which in Dagestan is a concept often more akin to chastity, is at the core of the image of an ideal Dagestani woman. "Intelligence" comprises devotedness, diligence, modesty, loyalty, and good upbringing.

A Dagestani woman is taught from an early age to be a hostess, a mother, and a guardian of the home. A woman's honor is carefully protected by her parents and brothers until she is married. A Dagestani woman is often subjected to the more traditional demands of being modest, obedient, and patient. She is expected to serve and honor her husband and please her mother-in-law. A young woman must also agree with the decisions made by other family members and to abide by family rules.

Despite these tightly defined expectations, women have always occupied a place of honor in Dagestani society. In the past, a woman could stop a bloody fight, rushing into the middle of it with her head uncovered and her hair loose, waving a handkerchief. Today, men watch their language when they are next to a woman, no matter how old she is. Furthermore, women gain authority and status with the passing of time and the attainment of old

The horse has been central to Dagestan's rural and mountain dwellers for centuries. Even today, some remote mountain villages can be accessed only on horseback. Traditionally, a guest, upon arriving, first offered praise to the host's horse. In the past, some ethnic groups killed a horse after the death of its owner.

age. Elderly women participate in decision making as much as men do. When an elderly woman enters the room, men get up from their seats to show their respect.

In the 20th century, during the Soviet era, women received more rights than ever before. Many Dagestani women pursued advanced degrees, started working outside of the home, and occupied positions at the middle and, albeit more rarely, higher administrative levels. At present, although there are women employed in government posts, they are heavily under-represented. In the fields of education and medicine, women represent the majority. Nevertheless, even those working outside the home are typically responsible for taking care of their children, for cooking, and for performing household chores. Thus, most Dagestani women bear a heavy workload.

Economic hardships make it necessary for some Dagestani men to move to other parts of Russia. While some do only seasonal work, others leave their families for longer periods of time. The migration of male workers also takes place within the republic. Those living in rural or mountain communities, unable to find work close to their homes, move to the plains or to urban areas. As a result, more and more often, a woman becomes the head of the family and, while the men are away, the primary breadwinner.

PARTOU PATIMA

In 1396, when the Mongols invaded Dagestan, a Lak woman named Partou Patima played a key role in the popular uprising against Timur. Her heroism is celebrated in songs and legends. Her name, a permanent part of Dagestan's history, has been a popular choice for newborn girls for centuries.

RESPECT FOR AGE

Dagestani children learn to respect not only their parents but all elders. They are taught to view the older members of their communities as a source of wisdom and experience. Thus, in light of this, older people are accorded a special place in Dagestani society. They are the first to be served food and the first to speak. Their advice is considered of the utmost importance and is usually heeded by those seeking counsel and direction.

In public transportation, young people typically give up their seats to elderly passengers. People also avoid smoking in the presence of the elderly. Disrespect for the elderly is frowned upon and is heavily criticized. The phrase "Let your old age be not needed by anyone!" is among the gravest insults. "Let God give you a long life for us!" is what an elder would prefer to hear instead.

Community elders are afforded a position of honor and respect in Dagestani society.

Opposite: **Ancient tomb-stones at an Islamic cemetery.**

CENTENARIANS

Dagestan is known for having many centenarians, people who are at least 100 years old. Most centenarians live in the intermediary mountain ranges, which are those at an altitude of 5,250 to 6,560 feet (1,600 to 2,000 m) above sea level, but centenarians can be found across the republic. The elders are revered by the whole community, much less their extended family, which consists of their children, grandchildren, and great-grandchildren. These century-old individuals are often praised for their good memory and bountiful sense of humor. Many demonstrate an exuberant zest for living and are often eager to give advice to the young.

According to the Russian census of 2002, three women in Dagestan turned 122 years old in that year. That means that in the 21st century young Dagestanis can listen to stories from those who grew up at the end of the 19th century.

DEATH RITUALS

Elders who feel that their own death is impending often organize their own memorial and prepare their own grave. Following Islamic tradition, the deceased is buried in a white piece of cloth before sunset on the day of the death. Someone who dies in the afternoon is buried the next day. If the death occurs in a room, the room is smoked to purify it, and all of its contents are brought outside into the sunlight. Distant relatives tend to visitors who come to express their condolences. In some ethnic groups, women visit in the morning, while men visit in the afternoon.

A funeral procession follows the body to the cemetery. Also according to Islamic practice, women follow the coffin only a short distance because they are not allowed to be present at the burial. Women offer up songs of mourning, often accompanied by tears. Men are not allowed to cry in public. The family of the deceased orders a *zikriad* (zee-kree-AHD), or funeral prayer, which is intoned in Arabic on the grave. A part of this prayer is repeated more than 7,000 times. After the funeral, the prayer is read in the house of the deceased. Then a memorial meal is served separately for the men and the women.

Villagers cancel all celebrations until the family of the deceased gives its consent for them to resume. If a young person dies, villagers will not celebrate weddings until an acceptable amount of time has passed. The immediate family of the deceased wears for some time the clothes they had on at the moment of their relative's death. Women usually dress in black, and men do not shave. Elderly women wear a dark-colored headpiece, and elderly men wear a *papakha* (pah-PAH-khah), a traditional tall astrakhan hat. Memorial days are observed on the third, seventh, and 40th days, and then one year after death.

Slavs bury their dead in coffins, usually on the following day or within two days after the death. Those who come to express their condolences or attend the funeral are offered candy. Christians invite a priest or a religious figure to read a prayer over the deceased. Memorial observances are marked on the ninth and 40th days after the death.

RELIGION

ISLAM, CHRISTIANITY, AND JUDAISM are the three major religions practiced in Dagestan. Islam is the dominant faith. More than 90 percent of the population is Sunni Muslim. Shiites are represented mostly by Azeris and Muslim Tats. Russians, Ukrainians, and Belarusians tend to be Orthodox Christians. There are also small groups of Baptists and other Protestant followers in the north. Armenian Gregorians and Catholics tend to cluster in the republic's urban areas. In addition, vestiges of the region's ancient folk religions are widespread.

A HISTORY OF BELIEFS

Different religions have contributed to the spiritual development of the Dagestani people. In the fourth and fifth centuries, Orthodox Christianity penetrated Dagestan from Byzantium, Armenia, Georgia, and Caucasian Albania. Nevertheless, the local population remained unconverted. In parts of Dagestan where some groups eventually came to accept Christianity, the new religion was for some time combined with old pagan rites, though eventually this hybrid belief system disappeared.

Judaism became firmly established in Dagestan in the fifth and sixth centuries with the arrival of the Tat-speaking Jews from Iran. The faith was supported by the Khazar Khanate. Although Judaism became a state religion in the Khazar region in the eighth century and took root in northern Dagestan, it never became widespread. The fall of the Khazar Khanate around 965 reduced the influence and practice of the religion in the future republic. Today, this religion is practiced by Mountain Jews and Dagestan's Ashkenazi Jews, who emigrated from Russia in the 1800s.

Islam took approximately a thousand years to establish itself in the region. The Arab expansion in the seventh century brought Islam to

A new mosque in the city of Gimerso. Many new mosques were built or old ones reopened in Dagestan after the fall of the Soviet regime.

Derbent. From there it spread to the southern and southeastern parts of Dagestan. In western Dagestan, Islam became prominent only in the 15th to the 17th centuries. As Islam became increasingly important, the influence of native and pagan religions was reduced. Over time many pagan beliefs merged with Islamic traditions. Islam became even more strongly rooted in Dagestan when foreign mullahs were gradually replaced by local ones.

Sufism and the Sufi order *nakshbandia* also played a role in the region's gradual embrace of Islam. Sufism is a mystical branch of Islam that accentuates internal belief. Sufism was used for political purposes by imams during the Caucasian War and began taking shape as a religious and political doctrine under Imam Shamil. During his rule, the idea of attaining a mystical understanding of God through a spiritual quest partly lost its influence. *Sharia*, only one of the steps of the ascent to God according to the tenets of Sufism, prevailed, and *gazavat*, armed defense and struggle against the unfaithful, was emphasized. This particular aspect of Sufism soon led to a religious zeal that swept the region.

Islam continued to flourish in Dagestan despite the victory of czarist Russia in the Caucasian War in the mid-19th century. In 1861 Dagestan had 1,628 registered mosques and 4,000 mullahs. By the beginning of the 20th century, there were more than 2,000 mosques. One of Dagestan's main printing houses of the time, in the town of Temir-Khan-Shura (present-day Buynaksk), published religious books in *ajam*. Based on Arabic script, *ajam* allowed for books to be published in local languages.

The Russian Revolution of 1917, however, brought this religious development to an end, and all religions were equally affected by the ensuing political changes. Churches, synagogues, and mosques were either closed or destroyed. Islamic religious schools ceased to exist, and thousands of mullahs were barred from practicing their faith if not executed. By 1985 there were only 27 officially functioning mosques, five churches, and three synagogues left in Dagestan. Nonetheless, dozens of underground religious institutions continued to function "illegally" throughout the Soviet era.

PAGANISM

Despite the long Islamic tradition and the framework of the monotheistic, or single deity, religions that became established in the region, Dagestani culture carries many traces of its pagan roots. Some Dagestanis, when they turn to God for help, perform pagan rituals often accompanied by Islamic prayers.

Paganism has left its mark on agricultural practices as well. Some ethnic groups perform rituals to fight the drought and to increase the harvest. These practices are found especially in the more rural precincts. In such a rite, one of the villagers who is believed to be "marked by God"—either through a physical handicap or particularity, as an only child in a family, or as the poorest person in the village—is undressed and covered with grass and green branches. A procession of young people attaches a rope to the chosen person and walks him through the village, joining in a special song about rain.

Instead of a person, some ethnic groups use a doll named Zemire, or Andir-shopai, an old name for the god of rain. If this rite is ineffective, villagers find the bones of a horse and bring them to a mullah. The mullah then reads two prayers: one asking God to send water from the sky and the other asking him to provide plenty of water in the wells. After the prayer, people take the bones to a well and wash them. The bones should not be immersed in water; otherwise it will never stop raining.

Pagan beliefs also designate certain areas and places as sacred. In southern Dagestan, a grave of a saint is called *pir* (PEER). In the north, it is called *zyarat* (zy-ah-RAHT). There are several hundred such graves, crowned with cube-shaped mausoleums. These graves can be seen from a distance, marked by long sticks with flags and pieces of colorful material attached to them. Those who are ill pray at the sacred sites for good health. Childless women may come to seek the blessing of pregnancy, while other believers seek out the sites in search of good luck.

THE ISLAMIC REVIVAL

With more than half of all of Russia's Islamic organizations located in Dagestan, the republic is seen as a bastion of the faith. There are 10 to as much as 100 times the number of restored Islamic institutions in Dagestan than in the other Islamic republics of Russia. More than 1,500 mosques and several thousand prayer houses have opened in Dagestan since the collapse of the USSR. Many of the mosques are found in rural areas. Of the newly restored mosques, 1,462 are located in villages and

Muslims attend a service at the main mosque in Makhachkala.

132 in cities. The number of mosque-connected communities, *jamaats*, rose 64 times between 1985 and 2001. Mosques run 245 primary schools and 132 middle schools. Forty-four branches of Islamic higher educational establishments attract Muslim students from across Russia.

The revival of Islam is especially strong in the central and northern parts of Dagestan. On Fridays, men above the age of 14 gather in mosques. Nearly all villagers, except for pregnant women, the sick, and small children, fast during the month of Ramadan. Villagers try to avoid those who break the fast or skip the Friday prayer sessions. Thus individuals often take part in religious rites and keep up with their faith on account of social pressure. Those who openly refuse to follow religious traditions can lose their right to be buried in the village cemetery.

In the south, however, the situation is different. Some villages have no restored mosques and no one to organize Friday prayers and sermons. Therefore, in some Lezgin, Lak, and Tabasaran villages, the function of mosques is replaced by sacred places, such as the sacred mountain

Shalbuzdag. In comparison with the Soviet era, the number of sacred places in the republic has increased from 127 to 836.

The hajj (pilgrimage to Mecca) and *umra* (small pilgrimage) have become increasingly popular since the 1990s. Although Dagestani Muslims make up only 10 percent of the Muslim population of Russia, in some years they have made up to 80 percent of all hajjis. In some villages, 20 to 40 percent of the population has made a hajj in the past decade. Minibuses, decorated with Arabic writings and Saudi souvenirs, regularly travel via Iran, Turkey, Syria, and Jordan to bring hajjis to Saudi Arabia. To avoid accidents, bus drivers make stops at sacred places to pray with the passengers for a safe trip.

A branch of Islam called Wahabbism has considerably destabilized Dagestan in the past 10 years. Followers of Muhammad ibn Abd al-Wahab, Wahabbites are Sunni radicals and extremists fighting to spread their

A Dagestani pilgrim sells glassware in Amman, Jordan, on his way home from Mecca.

particular vision and interpretation of Islam. The movement originated in Saudi Arabia and is especially active in neighboring Chechnya. In Dagestan, in particular, they oppose Sufism. The conflict between Wahabbites and Sufis reached a crisis point in 1997. Two years later, extremist units invaded the Botlikh, Tsumada, and Novolak regions of Dagestan from the territory of Chechnya. In September 1999, the Dagestani parliament adopted a law banning the Wahabbites and other extremist organizations from the republic. Nonetheless, the Wahabbites, receiving significant financial support from Saudi Arabia and other places, persist in their activities.

The Islamic revival, however, has been stabilizing or losing force since the late 1990s. The demand for Islamic literature has fallen, and the number of pilgrimages, as well as primary schools run by mosques, has decreased. Islamic culture, flourishing in Dagestan before and immediately after the demise of the Soviet Union, has not been able to revive fully.

Muslims pray at the old mosque in the village of Echeda.

LANGUAGE

Opposite: **Signs advertise products and services offered along a commercial street in Makhachkala.**

WITH 14 MAJOR LANGUAGES and dozens of dialects spoken within its borders, Dagestan is the most multilingual republic of the Russian Federation. Within a small territory, 2 million people speak the tongues of three major language families: Indo-European, Caucasian, and Turkic. The prevalent languages—Avar, Dargin, Lezgin, Kumyk, Lak, Azeri, Russian, Tabasaran, Chechen, and Nogay—are spoken by the republic's largest ethnic groups. With some exceptions, Dagestani languages are characterized by a great number of consonants and very few vowels.

Today most Dagestanis are multilingual. They speak the language of their ethnic group, the local language of inter-ethnic communication (such as Avar, Kumyk, or Azeri), the Russian language, and sometimes the language of their neighbors (Chechen or Georgian). Russian is the undisputed lingua franca in Dagestan, the common language used by a wide variety of groups most commonly for government affairs and to transact business. Replacing the Roman alphabet with the Cyrillic alphabet in 1938 made Russian more accessible. In 1989, 61 percent of Dagestanis spoke Russian.

After Russian, Avar is the second most common language of inter-ethnic communication and the native language of 99 percent of Avars. The Avar language belongs to the northern Caucasian language family. The number of dialects is so great that practically every village has its own. The literary language is based on the so-called "language of the guest," which has developed through the centuries via conversations with guests and in markets where residents of different villages interacted. Before Arabic *ajam*, the Avars used the Georgian and the Albanian writing systems. Five Dagestani languages—Avar, Dargin, Lak, Lezgin, and Tabasaran—have literary status, while others exist only in spoken form.

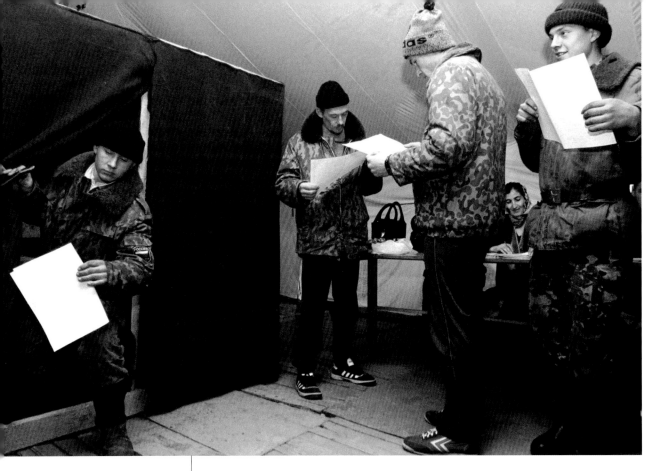

Russian soldiers study their ballots as they wait to cast their votes at a polling station in Botlikh.

The evolution of Dagestan's various languages is unique. For more than 4,000 years, many of the nation's dialects and tongues have been spoken in many of the same locations where they are still in use today. One explanation as to why so many distinct Caucasian dialects and tongues have been preserved is that their native speakers lived in scattered groups that had little contact with one another. Even the residents of some neighboring mountain villages—separated by deep and impassable gorges—often speak different languages. Some indigenous languages are spoken by no more than a few hundred people and are in danger of dying out.

THE ALPHABET

The frequent changes to the writing systems used in Dagestan reflect its rich and turbulent linguistic history. At different times, cuneiform, the Caucasian Albanian alphabet, Gunn writing, Khazar writing, Arabic *ajam*, the Roman alphabet, and the Cyrillic alphabet have been used.

Caucasian Albanian, one of the two indigenous Caucasian alphabets, went out of use early in the region's history. Although scholars knew about the existence of this alphabet starting at the end of the 19th century, it only became an object of study half a century later, after the discovery of copies of the Caucasian Albanian alphabet used in 15th- and 16th-century Armenian manuscripts. Short writing on a stone slab in Azerbaijan was discovered as well.

Due to Dagestan's long tradition of Islamic culture and literature, many Dagestani languages were written in Arabic script. The oldest example of this kind is a group of notes in the Dargin language, written on the margins and between the lines of an Arabic manuscript from A.D. 1243. Other examples of writing in Arabic script, as well as in Dargin, Lak, and Avar, date back to the 15th century. The Arabic alphabet *ajam* was used in Dagestan until 1928, when it was replaced by the Roman alphabet. In 1938 the Roman alphabet was replaced by the Cyrillic alphabet. Although Dagestanis usually learned to read and write in their own languages, most also mastered Russian as a second language. The Cyrillic alphabet, which was introduced at the time and which is still used, included the letter I, which existed in the pre-revolutionary Russian alphabet. Since this was the only letter that was added, some consonants in Dagestani languages are rendered through the combination of several Russian letters.

THE MEDIA

Dagestan's mass media also reflect the republic's multilingualism. More than 200 print and electronic media outlets and sources are available and produced in Dagestan's various languages. While some print media are published in one language, others are translated into a range of languages. State television and radio stations broadcast in 12 languages.

A teacher presents a chemistry lesson to high-school students in Agvali. Russian remains the language of instruction in Dagestan's schools, although federal law recognizes the right of minority groups to preserve their native languages.

The majority of print media are controlled to some extent by the state. Administrative bodies on all levels use newspapers for disseminating information and conveying political purposes and intent. The state radio of Dagestan recently celebrated its 75th anniversary. Television has existed in Dagestan since the 1960s, and today, there are both state and commercial channels. A wide range of Islamic media outlets exists in Dagestan. Some channels interrupt broadcasting during prayer. Most religious mass media cover social and political issues. Given the complex political situation in the Caucasus, the Muslim Spiritual Administration controls all religious mass media.

Print media circulation has shrunk drastically in recent years. Twenty years ago, 750 newspaper copies were printed for every 1,000 people living in the republic, in contrast to only 160 today. Total weekly newspaper circulation has gone down from 1.5 million to 320,000 copies. While Russian and Avar print media suffered the greatest loss of readership, other language media have survived, often thanks to special state funding.

GREETINGS AND GESTURES

Greetings and gestures play a crucial role in the day-to-day communications of Dagestanis. Over centuries, the social mores and conventions of different ethnic groups, typically sharing similar economic or religious backgrounds, have converged. Dagestani codes of behavior emphasize the demonstration of respect for elders and the difference between the social roles of men and women. In addition, special behavioral norms exist for communication on bridges and at malls, public ovens, bathing places, and streams.

When asked "How are you?", a Dagestani always answers "Fine." Social practice dictates that people should not complain. Nor should they demonstrate that they are tired or bored, thirsty or hungry. When talking to someone, it is important for Dagestanis to stay friendly and calm. While working, people especially attempt to display a good attitude or mood. It is also deemed important for a person not to emphasize his or her personal input to a given task or project, and it is considered in poor taste to comment on or compare another's work. In addition, employees look for ways to alleviate the work load or burden of others.

In rural areas, women and men, especially those who are not married, are expected to keep a respectful distance from one another. Therefore communication between female and male villagers is often limited to a short greeting, sometimes followed by a question about the well-being of family members.

Gestures intensify the meaning of spoken words. Dagestanis often use them to express anger. Slapping one's hips and pinching express disdain, while pointing one's hands to the sky and then covering the face with them express disappointment and contempt. Placing the hands on the hips and raising one's chest express superiority and independence.

Communication on horseback has its own special rules. When meeting or crossing paths, riders are expected to show respect by rising halfway in the saddle. Meeting an older person, a rider slows down, rises in the saddle, and silently passes by, acknowledging that person with a glance. Meeting someone familiar, the rider dismounts the horse, takes off his hat, and greets with a handshake and friendly words.

ARTS

LITERATURE, ARCHITECTURE, ropewalking, body tattooing, theater, and painting all reflect Dagestan's lively and diverse artistic traditions. The decorative arts occupy a major place in Dagestan's cultural heritage. Traditionally, villages specialized in one type of decorative art, and many still do: Gotsatl is famous for its silverware, Balkhar its pottery, Untsukul its wood carvers, Khuchni its carpet makers, and Kubachi its jewelry.

Excavations in different parts of the republic have shown that bronze was already widely used by jewelers 5,000 years ago. Fathers passed the secrets of their trade to their sons; mothers passed their craftmaking skills to their daughters. Historians and travelers from around the world admire the beauty and craftsmanship of Dagestani handiwork, and for many years the work of Dagestani craftspeople has been exhibited in museums around the world.

CARPET MAKING

Dagestan is known around the world for its carpets. In response to the increased availability of mass-produced carpets that often replicate the traditional designs, women in the village of Tabasaran are preserving the republic's long tradition of handwoven carpets.

The Dagestani art of carpet making dates back to ancient times. The oldest still-existing Dagestani carpet was made in the sixth century in Derbent. In the past, masters brought their carpets to the shores of the Caspian Sea. They believed that their work was complete only when the carpet had been washed by the sea waves and warmed in the sun. For centuries, light and thin carpets featuring different shapes, designs, and motifs—mostly in blue and red—have been an essential part of any Dagestani home.

Opposite: **Traders spread out their carpets at a bazaar in Derbent.**

KUBACHI JEWELRY

In ancient times, the 2,000-year-old village of Kubachi was famed for making armor and chain mail. Three hundred years ago, it excelled in making daggers, swords, pistols, and guns. Today Kubachi is renowned for its jewelry. No place in the Caucasus can boast such excellent and delicate engraving techniques. Sometimes, black ornament appears on a light silver background or vice versa.

The home of every master has a small museum or display highlighting examples of jewelry and pottery work from the past. While some of these works were made locally, others were brought from India and

A display of Kubachi daggers. Their hilts are ornately decorated with jewels, bone, and niello designs.

the Middle East. Exquisite scabbards and the hilts of old armaments, filigree jewelry, cigarette cases, wine vessels, caskets, goblets, vases, and trays all find their admirers in different parts of the world. The works of Kubachi masters have been exhibited in Saint Petersburg, Moscow, Brussels, Montreal, Osaka, and London. In 1937 Kubachi goldsmiths won the Grand Prix in Paris.

BALKHAR POTTERY

The Lak village of Balkhar has specialized in ceramics since the 13th century. Originally emerging in the mountains as a simple means of earning a living, Balkhar ceramics turned into an art form. People from across the Caucasus bought the beautiful pottery made by the villagers.

Taught from an early age, Balkhar women were responsible for the entire pottery-making process, from finding the clay to firing a completed work in the oven or kiln. Men helped prepare the clay, repaired the ovens, and brought the finished pottery to the market and either sold it or exchanged it for other goods, usually from other parts of Dagestan or from Azerbaijan.

Balkhar residents make around 30 kinds of kitchenware, each with its own function: carrying water, heating milk, whipping butter, pickling cheese, or storing flour or grain. Kitchenware, diverse in its design, is distinguished by its rich ornamentation, thin walls, fine lines, and symmetrical forms. Potters coat their works with yellow and white clay. White clay tends to turn red after the heating process.

Spirals, scrolls, and curves, as well as scenes of life in the mountains, embellish the distinctive pottery of the Balkhar residents. More recently, Balkhar masters have started making decorative plates and miniature statuettes as well.

UNTSUKUL WOOD CARVING

Although wood carving has been popular nearly everywhere in Dagestan, the village of Untsukul has won special fame in this area of expertise. For 200 years Untsukul masters have been developing unique methods of decorating spoons, plates, and walking sticks. More recently, Untsukul craftspeople have started making frescoes adorned with plant and animal designs. These frescoes are typically used as home decoration.

TSOVKRA ROPEWALKING

"Ballet on a rope" is what Parisian newspapers wrote with admiration about the ropewalkers who brought fame to the tiny mountain village of Tsovkra. There, according to popular lore, the day of a boy's birth is when he starts learning how to walk on a rope. According to legend, Tsovkra men stretched ropes over a precipice to shorten the way to goat and sheep pastures. With the passing of years, ropewalking turned into an art form.

A ropewalker, dancing a *lezginka* (lez-GHEEN-ka) on a thin cord, is an essential part of any Dagestani feast. As it was done centuries ago, brave men balance on a steel rope high above the ground, performing dangerous tricks without any safety measures, to the strains of *zurna* (zoor-NAH) and drums. The most spectacular trick is *farmingo* (fahr-MEEN-goh), in which four men stand on one another's shoulders and perform a back flip with their eyes covered.

DANCE

In Dagestan the ability to dance is highly prized. In the past, when strict laws did not allow for free and open communication between the sexes before marriage, dances at weddings were an opportunity for young people to establish contact and to express their interests in and feelings for one another. Certain gestures and glances carried special meanings. As dancing was believed to demonstrate one's dignity and dexterity, dancers were observed by potential in-laws.

The most famous dances are the *lezginka* and the saber dance. A saber dance features an explosion of nonstop energy. Men move around the stage, clinking their sparkling sabers with speed and precision.

Lezginka, arguably the most famous folk dance in the post-Soviet era, is an echo of older, pagan rituals in which eagles had a special meaning. The image and symbolism of the bird is portrayed by the male dancer when he balances on his toes, spreads his arms (to signify wings), and

An Avar woman and a Chechen man dance together in the village of Rahata in the Botlikh area of Dagestan.

then circles them, as if preparing to soar. Dances performed by women are marked by grace and dignity. In contrast to the sharp, tempestuous movements of the men, the women look as if they are floating on air, moving gracefully and smoothly across the floor. In some dances, the woman cannot raise her hands higher than her waist. Only rarely can she throw a glance at her partner. The man looks at the woman as if he is trying to protect her. Throughout the dance, though, the overriding rule is that the man can never touch the woman.

BODY TATTOOING

Body tattooing is one of the oldest traditions practiced by some ethnic groups living in the mountains of Dagestan. It serves several functions. Some tattoos were made to mark a woman as belonging to a certain clan or ethnic group. Other tattoos were used to show her age. Girls aged 13 to 15 were tattooed to indicate that they had entered the age of puberty. Tattoos were placed on the face, hands, arms, legs, feet, or breasts. Quite often tattooing had ritual and mystical meaning. For others it was simply a form of decoration. Although each ethnic group and each village had its own tattooing patterns, plants and animals were the most frequent motifs.

ARCHITECTURE

Most Dagestani cities and towns resemble stereotypical Russian urban centers, full of apartment blocks that can hardly be differentiated from one another. This style and model of urban planning was followed throughout the 20th century. What preceded this prevalent aesthetic, though, the traditional architecture of Dagestan's mountain villages, demands a closer look.

Mosques, watchtowers, signal towers, fortresses, and bridges dominate the Dagestani architectural landscape in the rural and mountainous communities. A number of arches and columns also characterize the architectural style. The wooden or stone façades of houses, mosques, and tombs are often carved. Despite the fact that Islam prohibits the images of people and animals from being portrayed, the carvings often depict beasts and birds, as well as hunting and fighting scenes. Special attention was traditionally given to the decoration of gates, often arch-shaped portals covered with traditional ornamentation. The entrances to some houses included inscriptions marking the date of the building's construction.

Dagestani architecture has been largely shaped by geography and the need of local residents to defend themselves from attacks. The key principles of house construction have stayed all but unchanged for centuries. Since early times, Dagestani villages, called *aoul* (ah-OOL), have been founded high in the mountains and often look like an extension of their natural settings. Since there was little land that could be used for agriculture and grazing, people settled on the southern sides of gorges and rocks. Rectangular-shaped houses were built of stone, clay, brick, and wood. Village construction did not follow any specific plan, so as to save space and to confuse attackers who would have trouble finding their way around the unfamiliar village. Normally, houses had one or two floors and a covered yard. Because of the lack of space, every square inch was utilized, and the flat roof of one house could serve as a neighbor's outdoor area or terrace. The ground floor of a house was

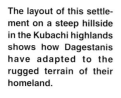

The layout of this settlement on a steep hillside in the Kubachi highlands shows how Dagestanis have adapted to the rugged terrain of their homeland.

usually reserved for household purposes. The southern sides of houses often had built-in galleries, balconies, or loggias, which were sometimes protected with glass.

Looking at a village located on a faraway hill, the houses mirror the surface of the terrain, forming ascending rows like a giant staircase. In a village on a mountainous plateau, houses are built next to one another, assuming the shape of an amphitheater. A narrow upward-curving street often has steps cut out of the stone. Here and there, streets smoothly turn into tunnels, going through the ground floors of buildings, and sometimes gradually making their way toward narrow arched bridges.

One of the primary concerns in building a house was the ability to defend it. Villages were designed to be inaccessible to enemies. As a rule only one path led to a village, and it was protected and guarded by lookouts stationed in a watchtower. Some houses were built as towers and fortresses, reaching high into the sky. For safety purposes, such fortresses were built without windows. A large stone wall surrounded all household constructions, forming a single complex that was easy to defend. From the outside, all that was visible were blank walls and a tiny entrance. The back side of the structure typically faced an abyss or bordered a wall of rock. Some constructions were interconnected by underground walkways.

Villages still look quite similar to how they did in the past. Terraced fields hug the mountainsides, gardens grow among rocks, and sheep make their way along narrow paths above the abyss. While the setting can be beautiful and tranquil, life is hard high in the mountains, where the soil is so stony it is difficult to coax crops from it.

Although today Dagestan has instituted a program that resettles people from mountain communities to the plains, residents of these often hard-to-reach high-altitude settlements are in no hurry to leave their ancestral homes. Even suggesting that someone should leave the mountains for a new life on the plains can be taken as an offence. Local lore states that a son once came back from the city to his village to talk his old father into moving down to the plains. "You would be better off stabbing my stomach with a sword than torturing me with such words," the old mountain resident answered.

FOLKLORE

Opposite: **The esteemed poet Rasul Gamzatov (1923–2003) wrote in Avar, his native language, but he drew a large following in Russia as well. His works won major prizes in the USSR.**

Dagestani folklore reflects the strong dual influences of Islam and paganism. Islamic beliefs coexist and often merge with tales about hobgoblins, forest creatures, and a variety of demons. A story tells of a female demon meddling in the birth of a child. Demons of disease are believed to make people sick. Homes and cemeteries also have their share of resident demons. The Dagestani have plenty of rites and songs

A DAGESTANI FOLKTALE

The prince of the Subterranean Kingdom fell in love with a girl from Earth. The loving couple got married and decided to escape from the kingdom. The furious king ordered his subjects to catch the runaways. When the young couple saw the people pursuing them, they asked God to turn them into a mosque with a mullah. Their wish came true, and the king's people, having found nothing on Earth but a mosque with a mullah, returned to the Subterranean Kingdom.

The king realized that his son had fooled him and ordered that the pursuit be resumed. However, the pursuers returned to report that this time they had not seen anything on Earth but a couple of ducks on a lake. The king realized he had been fooled again. He issued the same proclamation, ordering the search party not to return without the runaways. When the young couple realized that they were still being pursued, they asked God to turn them into a boulder, and once again their wish came true. Since then people have been honoring the boulder and coating it with fat.

to protect themselves from evil spirits and to invite and welcome the more beneficial ones.

Tales, legends, and myths about unfortunate lovers, heroes, and fighters for independence teach young Dagestanis about codes of honor and dating rituals and encourage a better understanding of the history of their homeland.

Effendi Kapiev, an esteemed Dagestani writer of Lak origin, devoted his life to collecting folklore. At weddings and funerals, at fireplaces, and in workshops, he filled his notebooks with stories. Each page of his notebooks was filled with the folk wisdom of mothers and lovers, as well as the legends engraved on old daggers and somber gravestones.

LITERATURE

Between the ninth and 14th centuries, most Dagestani literary works were set down in Arabic. Some works were produced in Persian, Azeri, and Turkish. The literature created in the languages of Dagestan's various ethnic groups first started appearing in the 14th century. Since the 19th century, many works have been written in Russian. Unfortunately many key writings were lost because of the frequent changes to the alphabet.

"A poet is a peer of not only those living today, but those who have left and those who are to come to this earth," wrote Rasul Gamzatov, Dagestan's greatest poet, whose works have been translated into many languages. Born in the tiny mountain village of Tsada, Gamzatov became one of the most prominent Soviet poets.

Other pillars of Dagestani literature include Kosta Hetagurov, Kyazim Mechiev, Suleiman Stalsky, and Gamzat Tsadasa. In Dagestan, men of letters always enjoyed the highest authority and respect. Poems are cited in daily conversations and at celebrations, and some are turned into popular songs.

A theater in Makhachkala. There are several theaters in Dagestan, including the Russian, Avar, and Dargin drama theaters and the State Opera and Ballet Theater.

THEATER

Theater had not been an integral part of Dagestani culture until the beginning of the 20th century. The first official theaters were founded as the offshoots of amateur companies. Theater has since become an increasingly important part of Dagestani culture. Directors stage both classical plays and pieces written in local languages by modern Dagestani playwrights.

The opening of the Russian Drama Theater and the Kumyk Theater of Music and Drama was followed by the founding of the Avar, Dargin, Lak, and Lezgin theaters. Today, theatrical presentations are staged at the State Opera and Ballet Theater as well as in smaller Azerbaijani, Nogay, or Tabasaran theaters. The capital also offers the Children's Theater. The Museum of the History of Dagestani Theaters attracts, in particular, those with an interest in the history of performance in the republic.

PAINTING

Like theater, painting did not come into its own in Dagestan until the 20th century. One of the first artists to introduce Dagestan to Western painting and techniques was Halilbek Musayasul. A Dagestani who was educated in Germany, Musayasul combined the traditions of the East and the West. Most of his symbolic, often grotesque, works were based on Dagestani themes.

His paintings have been exhibited in the best museums in Turkey, Germany, France, and the United States. The Metropolitan Museum of Art in New York City exhibits a cast of the artist's hands. Unable for dozens of years to return home from living abroad, Musayasul bequeathed all his works to his homeland. Although the artist's ashes are preserved in New Jersey, his works have now returned to the land of his ancestors.

LEISURE

LIKE PEOPLE FROM ALL LANDS, Dagestanis love to socialize. No matter how busy they are, people strive to find time to spend with friends and family. While well-off city dwellers flock to restaurants, home is the most popular gathering place for most Dagestanis. On Sundays families usually visit their parents. Guests are typically invited for dinner once or twice a week. People drop by even without an invitation, as guests are always welcome.

In Dagestan, like nearly everywhere in Russia, women have less free time than men. They also usually spend more time with children than men do. Besides sometimes working outside the home, they are responsible for the domestic upkeep of the household. Socializing with other wives and mothers while performing their various daily tasks is a common activity in many Dagestani communities.

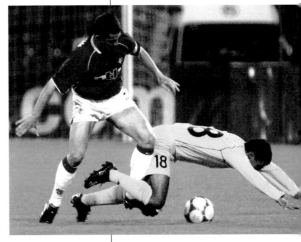

Above: **A player** *(in yellow)* **representing the capital city of Makhachkala hits the turf in an attempt to keep the ball from his Scottish opponent during a UEFA match.**

Opposite: **Shoppers browse through the varied merchandise of a covered market in Dagestan.**

CITIES

In cities people can attend concerts and exhibitions and watch plays or movies. People generally do not go out alone. They bring along friends or family. Staying at home or socializing at home is also a common pastime.

Young urbanites love surfing the Internet, playing video games, and watching videos and DVDs. Young people also go to movies and nightclubs. However, clubs and dancehalls generally have a lack of young women, as carousing and staying out late can damage a girl's reputation. Many young men spend a lot of time working on their physiques in gyms.

In summer families spend a lot of time outdoors. City parks, especially at the seaside, are filled with people talking, playing with children, reading, or locked in a heated chess match. Crowds gather next to chessboards, cheering the players on. Children and youth ask their parents for money for amusement-park-style rides. People also go to the countryside, where some families have small country houses. Hiking and a variety of outdoor sports have become increasingly popular.

VILLAGES

An all-male group passes the time together in the sunshine of Echeda.

Villagers tend to have less free time than urban residents, and rural areas offer few opportunities for entertainment. Like in cities, people spend a

large share of their free time watching television. Every village, no matter how large or small, has a cultural or community center, called the "house of culture" during the Soviet era. The activities offered in the centers depend on the village's financial standing. Most cultural centers function as the local library and the movie theater. Those that have more funds at their disposal sometimes have billiard tables. It is mostly young men who gather there in the evenings. Young women commonly visit the center during the day. During late or nighttime hours, they arrive only in the company of an elder brother or cousin.

MEETING PLACES

The most popular place for women of all ages to socialize and catch up is the public oven or the local water source. While talking there, they never put their heavy water jugs on the ground, as they do not want to be perceived by other villagers as being lazy and gossipy.

Men spend virtually all their free time on the *godekan*. A centrally located square, the *godekan* has many functions. First of all, it is where men develop socially, learning the qualities of *namus* and *yag'*. It is also a place where the older and younger generations meet. Elders also gather there, and thus it is the place where important community decisions are made. The elders, sitting on benches, watch young men playing sports. Locals also come to the *godekan* to meet friends, share news, get advice, play games, or sell goods. Travelers come to the square to find lodging. A *godekan*, however, is a men's club where women are not welcome.

In cities a *godekan* does not exist. Nonetheless, men born in rural areas attempt to create *godekan*-like enclaves in city parks. Old men sitting on benches try to engage in conversations with passersby or give advice to the young. Many townsfolk, however, find such behavior unusual.

SPORTS

Dagestanis joke that they rank first in the number of Olympic medals any nation has won in respect to the total population. At the Summer Olympic Games in Sydney and Athens, Dagestani freestyle wrestlers and boxers secured six gold, three silver, and four bronze medals. Wrestling in Dagestan has historic roots. The ongoing resistance to the various invasions that have shook the region fostered the development of martial arts and wrestling. Since early childhood, the typical Dagestani boy is brought up to be a defender. The stress placed on strength and physical prowess has contributed to the development of excellent wrestling schools. No feast in Dagestan is celebrated without a wrestling competition, both among men and boys. In addition Dagestani sportsmen have attained high international rankings in the martial arts, pistol shooting, and archery.

A volleyball match in Kvanada, Dagestan.

In a land where vigor is highly prized, successful and esteemed athletes have become heroes. In addition the republic takes pride in athletes of Dagestani origin who have won medals in the Olympic Games while representing Russia.

Two young athletes pit their strength and skill against each other in a wrestling competition in Kvanada, Dagestan.

SINGING

Dagestanis love singing and honor and praise their most talented singers. People sing at work, in their free time, and during celebrations. During winter, when the harvest is over, some villages host singing contests, which attract the best singers of the area. Previously only men were allowed to take part in these contests, but today women also participate. Folk songs—both religious and secular—were often performed as dialogues. A man would start, and a male choir would join in, repeating the refrain. Then a woman would answer the first singer, after which other women would pick up the tune. People sing without accompaniment or to the strains of the *buben* (BOO-ben), *chungur* (choon-GOOR), *tanbur* (tahn-BOOR), *zurna*, and *svirel* (svee-REHL)—the main Dagestani percussion, string, and wind instruments.

FESTIVALS

DAGESTANI FESTIVALS trace their roots not only to Islamic and folk traditions but to Russian and Soviet celebrations as well. Many of the republic's holiday customs and practices even reflect ancient Eastern religions. Islamic holidays are celebrated according to the Islamic calendar, and their dates shift each year. On Islamic holidays, believers go to the mosque for the public prayer and sermon. Folk holidays follow the rhythm of the agricultural calendar and can therefore be divided into spring, summer, and fall celebrations. Spring holidays symbolize the preparation prior to the work year and provide the last chance to relax before the hard work begins.

Spring and summer holidays unite the entire village community and often bear romantic or sentimental associations. The beauty of nature and the inviting temperatures of the summer months are conducive to entertainment, games, and sports competitions. In the fall Dagestanis celebrate the harvest with family and neighbors. Winter is the time to rest after the long hours of labor. It is the time for family celebrations and quiet evenings with friends and relatives.

During the Soviet era Dagestanis started celebrating the Russian New Year, International Women's Day (March 8), Victory Day (May 9) to mark the end of World War II, Labor Day (May 1), and the Socialist Revolution Day (November 7). At present the latter two events, like elsewhere in Russia, are celebrated only by a limited circle of people.

Above: **Dagestanis honor their war veterans on Victory Day in the Tsumada district.**

Opposite: **Dancers in traditional festive attire perform in a parade.**

115

A man chooses a ram
for the Kurban Bairam
sacrifice.

JUMA

The Juma day of Friday is a weekly Islamic holiday, equivalent to the
Sabbath day of Sunday for Christians and Saturday for Jews. On Friday
Muslims gather in a mosque for the special prayer and sermon. The
Prophet Muhammad chose that specific day as "the light of Islam" started
spreading on a Friday, and according to Islamic belief a Friday will be
the day the dead are resurrected. Although Friday is a work day in the
republic, religious Dagestanis dress up, cook special food, and visit
relatives and friends nonetheless.

KURBAN BAIRAM

Kurban Bairam (in Turkic), or Id al-Adha (in Arabic), is a day honoring
sacrifice to God and is one of the most honored holidays for Dagestani

Muslims. There are special and regular sacrifices. A special sacrifice may be made to fulfil a vow—perhaps in asking for a son—or as a public sign of repentance for sins. To demonstrate repentance the entire body of a sacrificial animal is given to the poor. In a regular sacrifice one-third of the meat goes to the family offering the sacrifice, and the rest is given to the poor.

Not only the celebration itself but also the process of preparing for it are intricate and ceremonial. A special service to God takes place in the mosques. People cook elaborate meals, consisting particularly of meat dishes, dress in their best clothes, and visit their family and friends to offer them presents. People also visit the graves of their ancestors and give alms. More and more, Kurban Bairam is celebrated by a growing circle of people.

MAVLID

The celebration of Mavlid, the Prophet Muhammad's birthday, became widespread in Dagestan only during the 1950s. Since no one knows the exact day when the prophet was born, Muslims celebrate his birthday throughout the month of *rabi ul-avval*.

Mullahs, familiar with the ceremony, stay quite busy during the month, as they are invited every day to visit different families. A mullah sings rhymes about the birth and life of Muhammad and about his glorious deeds. Every four lines, the group repeats a refrain.

The final part of the ceremony is *zikr*, where a soloist is accompanied by the group, singing a thousand times the words *La ilaha illallah*, meaning "There is no other God than Allah." People sit in a circle, rocking their heads left and right, sometimes reaching a trancelike state, which they come out of with the help of the mullah.

URAZA BAIRAM

Uraza Bairam, or Id al-Fitr in Arabic, celebrates the end of a 30-day period of lent. This is a second important Islamic holiday. However it typically occasions more joy than Kurban Bairam because it celebrates the end of a particularly tough period. The Uraza Bairam ceremony consists of a special public prayer followed by a meal that extends over several hours. On Uraza Bairam people visit their family and friends and exchange gifts. Dressed festively people take walks, visit the graves of their ancestors, and give alms to the poor.

NAVRUZ

March 21, the day of the vernal equinox, is celebrated by most Dagestanis as Navruz, or the Islamic New Year. Navruz is a celebration of life in which warmth and light win out over the forces of evil and the chill of the winter.

Dagestanis start preparing for Navruz well in advance. Women cook flour cereal, enough for several days, as it is commonly believed that the longer the cereal lasts the longer prosperity will stay in the house. Women also bake special bread in the shape of animals, birds, or people. This bread is given as a gift to the friends and relatives who come to visit the family in the evening. The villagers gather to eat and have fun. Girls tell fortunes, and young men compete in wrestling. The winner will have good luck in the new year.

Late at night each family lights a fire in the yard. In darkness the village, seen from afar, looks like a gigantic torch. Boys shoot little clay balls with burning twigs inside them. The sound of clay balls crackling in flight is believed to scare off evil spirits. People entertain themselves by jumping over fires that are thought to help spring gain its force. All sorrow and

Navruz has much in common with the ancient pagan rituals once performed by the local populations.

grief burn in the fire, and people step into the new year cleansed of evil and full of renewed hope. The ashes and coals from Navruz fires are collected and kept throughout the next year as a form of protection.

Dagestani Muslims crowd the mosques to pray as a community at the start of Ramadan, the Islamic month of fasting that ends in the celebration of Uraza Bairam.

THE FIRST FURROW

The celebration of the first furrow dates back to ancient times. Today it is a sophisticated ceremony, performed in various ways by the different ethnic groups. The main idea of the rite, however, is common to all. On the day of the vernal equinox rural residents come to the fields to make the first furrows. A ritual announces the beginning of the planting season and aims to secure an abundant harvest. Muslim ethnic groups invite mullahs to read prayers. The celebration continues with horseback riding, wrestling, and stone throwing.

DAY OF FLOWERS

The Day of Flowers is one of the year's most beautiful events. Previously it was celebrated only on Mount Chapar-Suv, where the Ahtyns concluded peace talks with their neighbors. The holiday has since been used to commemorate peace and even to appease enemies. It is celebrated on all mountains and hillsides that are dotted with wildflowers.

The young especially look forward to the Day of Flowers because it gives them a chance to meet someone from a different village and to make a connection that might potentially lead to marriage. Young men chosen by the elders compete in a 6-mile (10-km) race. They run up a hill or mountain, starting fires along the way. At night, dancing and singing, young Dagestanis carry torches up the hill to watch the sunrise from the mountaintop. At noon they go back to their villages, where they are greeted by the elders who do not take part in the celebration. The young give them flowers, after which they return to their homes.

CHERRY DAY

As soon as the cherries ripen, the word *karu* (kah-ROO), meaning "cherry," starts traveling from one *aoul* to another. Villagers gather in shady gardens to savor the first cherries of the year. People dance, sing, and compete in horseback riding contests.

CONSTITUTION DAY

The day the second constitution of Dagestan was adopted (July 26, 2003) is widely celebrated in the nation's urban areas. City residents dress up in old national costumes and dance, play games, or stroll in the central streets. At night fireworks illuminate the sky, and thousands of balloons in the colors of the Dagestani flag soar into the air and out of sight.

NEW YEAR

New Year's Day is one of the republic's most popular holidays. Preparation for the new year starts well in advance. Houses and streets are decorated with garlands and toys. Everyone buys New Year's presents and sends greeting cards to friends and family.

On December 31 Dagestanis part with the old year, leaving their sorrows in the past. Guests come in the evening and take seats at a table laden with food and drink. When the clock strikes 12 at midnight, everyone makes a wish, gets up from his or her seat, clinks glasses, and says, "New Year, New Happiness!" Eating and dancing then continue late into the night.

School groups march in a parade.

FOOD

GEOGRAPHY AND RELIGION have done much to shape Dagestan's national cuisine. For centuries most local peoples made bread, cereals, and soups out of the plants, meat, and dairy products available to them. Food choice, however, was generally limited because of the lack of arable land and pasture space.

Modern Dagestani food combines the thousand-year-old cooking traditions of indigenous ethnic groups with outside culinary influences. The Nogays and Kumyks gave Dagestani cuisine a Mongolian touch, the Tats, a Persian flavor. The remarkably diverse Azeri cuisine added variety to Dagestani food as well. The Russians, Ukrainians, and Belarusians brought, in turn, their own recipes and introduced potatoes, cabbage, and tomatoes. Developments during the Soviet era enriched Dagestani cuisine with candies, salads, macaroni, and canned and convenience foods. In addition people acquired new means of storing food as well as new types of kitchen utensils and appliances.

Religion has mainly shaped the nation's attitude to meat. Neither Muslims nor Jews eat pork; Jews do not eat horse meat either. Herds of sheep grazing on hillsides and in the mountains provide meat, the preferred choice of Dagestani Muslims and Jews, while Christians have no dietary restrictions.

MEALTIMES AND TABLE MANNERS

Mealtimes in Dagestan are social events. Food and drink seem to be secondary—it is the people that matter most.

Dagestanis eat three times a day. Breakfast is a quick light meal eaten early in the morning. Working people have lunch either at a cafeteria or drop by their home during their lunch break. Those with a free schedule

Opposite: **Customers browse as fruit vendors promote their produce at a market in Dagestan.**

Residents of the village Kvanada enjoy a communal, outdoor meal.

have lunch somewhere between 1 and 3 P.M. Later the family gathers for dinner, the main meal of the day.

A Dagestani meal consists of one course and a beverage. Because there is only one major dish, plates are usually filled with it. People are brought up from an early age to be reserved in eating. Gluttony is perceived as shameful. Besides, this tradition is shaped by the general lack of time. Women work hard throughout the day at their various duties and domestic chores and do not have the time to prepare several courses.

Certain table manners are important to know before visiting a Dagestani family. Because Dagestanis love guests, an outsider is offered food as soon as he or she enters the house. Dagestanis view the serving of guests as an honor. The elder members of the family usually take their seats first and are served first as well. Guests are seated according to their age and relative status. The head of the family begins the meal. In villages family members sometimes eat from a large central dish. At the table people try to be considerate. It is important to avoid staring at women or discussing their behavior, manners, or clothes.

Before each sip of an alcoholic drink, Dagestanis clink glasses and pronounce a long and often poetic toast. Making a toast is an art form, and people compete in the eloquence of their speeches. They raise glasses to love, health, happiness, and good luck and address their wishes to guests, parents, friends, or children. Drinking in the company of elderly people, a young person can empty the glass only after being asked repeatedly to do so. Important to Dagestani society is the attitude toward drunkenness and imbibing large amounts of alcohol. A simple unspoken rule prevails. As soon as a person feels tipsy, he or she should quietly leave the table.

DUMPLINGS

Hinkal (heen-KAHL), which is a plain dumpling with no filling, is the most popular Dagestani dish. Its variety of forms and tastes is beyond description. *Hinkal* varies in the flour used to make the dough, in the shape of the dumplings, and in the sauce drizzled over them or served on the side. Therefore, although *hinkal* is made all over Dagestan, experienced gourmets can tell the origin or home affiliation of the cook after a few quick bites.

Dumplings of all imaginable shapes and sizes are made of wheat, rye, barley, bean, or corn flour. Corn-flour *hinkal* is especially prevalent in the cuisines of Dagestanis, Chechens, and Kumyks. In Archib, however, where corn does not grow, corn-flour *hinkal* with fresh milk is considered a delicacy and is served only on special occasions.

With most ethnic groups, *hinkal* is served with garlic sauce and any of a number of dairy products: yogurt, sour milk, sour cream, butter, or cheese. Many people eat *hinkal* with fresh or dried meat or sausage. Avars, Dargins, and Agouls often dress *hinkal* with mutton fat. Kumyks serve *hinkal* with tomatoes and nuts, while Tats tend to prefer theirs with generous helpings of vegetables and fruit. Avari *hinkal* sometimes comes with *urbech*, a seasoning made either of slightly fried ground flax seeds mixed with butter and honey or of ground nuts mixed with fresh or dried apricots. Finally *hinkal* can be served in many different ways. Some cooks leave dumplings floating in the soup, while others serve them separately on a plate with a cup of bouillon, or broth, accompanying them.

Filled dumplings, referred to as *kurze* (koor-ZEH), *kazan borek* (ka-ZAHN boh-REHK), *pelmeni*, and *vareniki*, should not be confused with *hinkal*, which are dumplings without filling. Meat and cottage cheese are popular dumpling fillings. Russian *pelmeni* are exclusively stuffed with meat. Dargin dumplings are filled with poultry, spring onions, eggs, pumpkin, potatoes, carrots, or fresh and dried apricots. Tsakhours make a special filling by mixing milk with eggs, and nettles with nuts. Kumyk cuisine features dumplings filled with pumpkin, nettle, or liver. Ukrainians usually fill their *vareniki* with potatoes, cottage cheese, or cherries.

PIES

Pies such as *choudou* (choo-DOO), *burkiv* (boor-KEEV), and *pirogi* are a mainstay of Dagestani cuisine. Like dumplings, pies can differ in size and filling. The most popular fillings are meat and cottage cheese, followed by nettle and eggs. In addition Archins like their pies with mutton fat or liver. Avars also eat them with mutton fat, while Kumyks prefer liver or pumpkin. Laks make pies with pumpkin, sorrel, and goosefoot, a type of plant. Dargin pies come with an assortment of fillings. Pumpkin, potatoes, spring onions, carrots, and fresh and dried apricots are just some of the fruits and vegetables found tucked inside. Russians, Ukrainians, and Belarusians bake mushroom, fish, apple, plum, and cherry pies.

ETHNIC TASTES

Over the years the differences and distinctions among the cuisines of Dagestan's ethnic groups have slowly begun to erode. This development is especially apparent in the cities, where people have a wide assortment of food at their disposal in grocery stores and at markets.

In addition the country's urban centers tend to draw a more diverse blend of people; this contributes to the interchange and evolution of culinary practices. The influence of Russian cuisine has been particularly strong, and Russian dishes are now part of most people's daily diets. Nonetheless, despite the commonality in much modern Dagestani cooking, people still retain their traditional preferences and signature dishes.

INDIGENOUS PEOPLES AND THE TATS Among the Tats and the region's original settlers, daily foods include *binkal* and various pies, soups, and cereals. Lamb is the meat of choice, and mutton fat is added to many dishes. Some village residents dry meat and sausage for winter. Meat dishes, such as *shashlyk* (grilled lamb), *dolma* (grape leaves stuffed with meat and rice), and pilaf (a blend of rice and meat) are at the heart of Tat cuisine. The traditional cheese *brynza* (BRYN-zah), made of sheep's milk, is also popular. A variety of seasonings is used: pepper, caraway seeds, thyme, ground walnuts, barberries, and vinegar. Tats are renowned for their spices, pickles, marinades, and especially their hot pickled peppers.

A hearty Russian loaf stuffed with a combination of sturgeon and rice flavored with onions and herbs.

Tea is a favorite Tat beverage, including Kalmyk salty tea, as well as *bouza* (boo-ZAH) and *ayran* (ahi-RAHN). Creamy drinks are made from different types of yogurt. The Dargins from Kaitag make *musti*, a boiled muscat wine, and also brew raisin beer. Tats brew a distinctive liquor that is similar to ouzo or *araki*, a licorice-flavored liqueur.

KUMYKS Kumyk specialties include rice-, corn-, or wheat-flour cereal called *chilav* (chee-LAHV), and *sorpa* (sohr-PAH), or soup, made with beans, rice, noodles, or nettles. Kumyks also make *kuvurma*, a meat sauce, and *kuimak*, whipped eggs. Like other peoples of the Caucasus, Kumyks love *hinkal*, *kurze*, *choudou*, *dolma*, *shashlyk*, and pilaf. Kumyk desserts include halva, pancakes, and jams. Favorite drinks are Kalmyk salty tea, coffee, and cocoa, which is borrowed from the West.

NOGAYS Nogays are famous for *kouvyrdak* (koo-vyr-DAHK), or fried meat with onions, a meat-and-noodle dish called *beshbarmak* (besh-bahr-MAHK), *balyk* (bah-LYK) *sorpa*, or fish soup, and the sausages *kazy* and *toltyrma* (tohl-tyr-MAH). Nogays also love *shashlyk*, pies, and eggs. Nogay cuisine is notable for its wide array of beverages. *Nogay shai* (tea), *koumiss* (mare's milk), *suv* (sherbet), and yogurt—*yugurt*, *ayran*, and *bouza*—are commonly served at Nogay tables.

MOUNTAIN JEWS The Mountain Jews are known for their fish, lamb, and chicken dishes, which are generally served with rice and vegetables. Fish is eaten dried, pickled, smoked, fried, boiled, or stuffed. The Mountain Jews grow and pick various greens and season food with plums, cherry plums, sloes, onions, and garlic. Specialties are a meat-and-vegetable blend called *bugleme* (boog-leh-MEH), a meat-and-onion stew coated with eggs, called *khoe-gusht* (hoheh-GOOSHT), a type of *dolma* called *yapragy* (yah-prah-GY), *hinkal*, and pilaf. The food of Mountain Jews has been influenced by other regional cuisines, most notably Iranian and Azeri cuisines.

SLAVS The food of Dagestani Russians, Ukrainians, and Belarusians has been strongly influenced by local and native Dagestani cuisine. Slavs in Dagestan cook *kurze*, *dolma*, *shashlyk*, *hinkal*, and other local specialties. Traditional Slavic dishes are borsch, or red beet soup, *pelmeni*, or meat dumplings, pancakes, and *golubtsy*, or cabbage leaves stuffed with meat and rice. Potatoes, noodles, and cereals are common side dishes that remain popular as well.

A family in a Dagestani village bakes bread in a traditional oven.

NETTLE DUMPLINGS

1½ tablespoons butter
½ pound wheat flour
2 eggs
salt
1⅓ cups minced nettle leaves
¼ cup finely chopped onions
butter or sour cream

Heat the butter slowly, then skim the solids off the top. The clarified butter will be used later to fry the nettles and onions. To make the dough, mix the flour, eggs, and a pinch of salt. Set aside for half an hour, then roll out into a thin layer and cut into small pieces. To make the filling, wash the nettle leaves, being careful to protect your hands with gloves. Fry the nettle leaves and onions, adding salt to taste, in the clarified butter. Put a small amount of the filling on each piece of dough, fold the dough over, and seal the edges. Boil the filled dumplings until they rise to the surface. Serve hot with butter or sour cream.

SHASHLYK TARKI-TAU

1 cup lamb
1¾ tablespoons onions
salt and pepper
½ ounce vinegar
1½ tablespoons fat
⅓ cup wheat flour

1 ounce water
1½ tablespoons sliced onions
1½ tablespoons green onions
¼ cup sliced fresh tomatoes
2 teaspoons dill or parsley

Dice the meat into 1-ounce cubes. In a bowl, mix the meat cubes with 1¾ tablespoons onions and salt and pepper to taste. Sprinkle the mixture with vinegar. Set aside in a cool place for three or four hours, then fry in the fat. To make the dough, mix the flour, water, and a pinch of salt. Roll out the dough into a thin disk, and bake on a baking sheet at 350°F (177°C) for five to seven minutes. On a plate pile the prepared meat in the form of a pyramid, and cover with the baked dough. Garnish with the sliced and green onions, tomatoes, and herbs.

LEMON AND CARAWAY DRINK

1 quart water
⅓ ounce caraway seeds
3 ounces sugar
1 ounce lemon juice

Boil the water with the caraway seeds for five minutes. Filter the water. Add the sugar, and bring the water to a boil again. Stir in the lemon juice. Cool and serve.

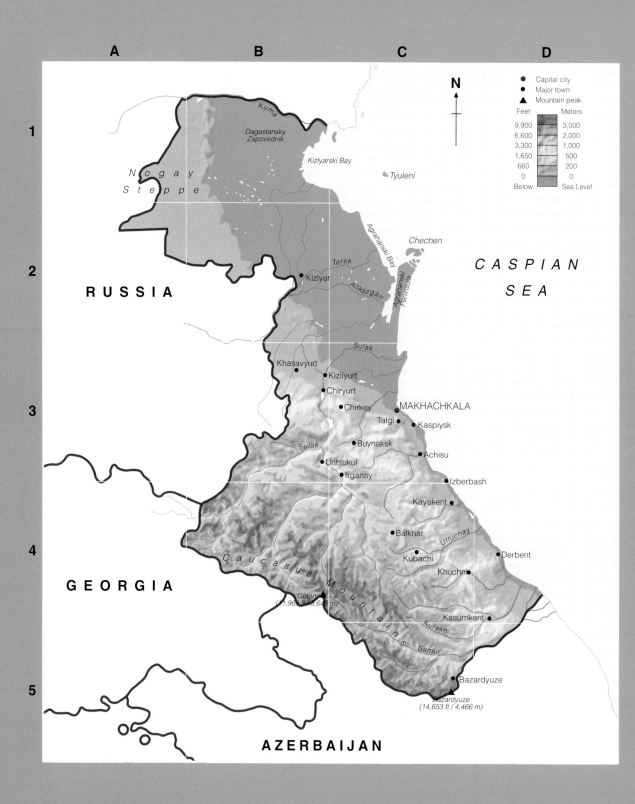

A   B   C   D

N

	Capital city
●	Major town
▲	Mountain peak

Feet		Meters
9,900		3,000
6,600		2,000
3,300		1,000
1,650		500
660		200
0		0
Below		Sea Level

1

Kuma

*Dagestansky
Zapovednik*

Kizlyarski Bay

N o g a y
S t e p p e

● *Tyuleni*

Chechen

C A S P I A N

S E A

Agrahanski Bay

2

R U S S I A

Terek

● Kizlyar

Alkazgan

*Agrahanski
Peninsula*

Sulak

Khasavyurt ●

● Kizilyurt

● Chiryurt

3

● Chirkey

Talgi ●

MAKHACHKALA

● Kaspiysk

Sulak

● Buynaksk

● Achisu

● Untsukul

● Irganay

● Izberbash

● Kayakent

Ulluchay

4

G E O R G I A

C a u c a s u s   M o u n t a i n s

● Balkhar

● Kubachi

● Khuchni

● Derbent

Guton
(11,965 ft / 3,648 m)

● Kasumkent

Kurakh

Samur

5

● Bazardyuze

*Bazardyuze
(14,653 ft / 4,466 m)*

A Z E R B A I J A N

MAP OF DAGESTAN

Achisu, C3
Agrahanski Bay, C2
Agrahanski
  Peninsula, C2
Alikazgan (river),
  B2, C2
Azerbaijan, A5,
  B4–B5, C4–C5,
  D4–D5

Balkhar, C4
Bazardyuze, C5
Bazardyuze, C5
Buynaksk, C3

Caspian Sea, B1,
  C1–C4, D1–D5
Caucasus Moun-
  tains, B4, C4–C5
Chechen (island),
  C2
Chirkey, C3

Chiryurt, B3

Dagestansky
  Zapovednik, B1
Derbent, D4

Georgia, A3–A5,
  B4–B5
Guton, B4

Irganay, C3
Izberbash, C3

Kaspiysk, C3
Kasumkent, D4
Kayakent, C4
Khasavyurt, B3
Khuchni, C4
Kislyarski Bay, B1,
  C1
Kizilyurt, B3
Kizlyar, B2

Kubachi, C4
Kuma (river), A1, B1
Kurakh (river),
  C4–C5, D4–D5

Makhachkala, C3

Nogay Steppe,
  A1–A2, B1–B2

Russia, A1–A4, B1,
  B2–B4, C1

Samur (river),
  C4–C5, D5
Sulak (river), B3, C3

Talgi, C3
Terek (river), B2, C2
Tyuleni (island), C1

Untsukul, B3

ECONOMIC DAGESTAN

Manufacturing

- Brandy
- Carpets
- Handicrafts
- Shipbuilding
- Textiles

Natural Resources

- Fish
- Hydroelectricity
- Oil

Farming

- Cattle

Services

- Port
- Tourism

ABOUT
THE ECONOMY

OVERVIEW

When the USSR collapsed, the new Republic of Dagestan had to figure out how to survive outside the Soviet framework that had supplied most of the demand and support for Dagestani industry. Dagestan's economy remains closely connected to that of Russia and has shrunk and grown more or less in tandem with it since 1991. Another major challenge that Dagestan faces in building its economy is an unstable political relationship with Chechnya.

Agricultural activity accounts for about 35 percent of Dagestan's annual earnings; machinery manufacturing and food processing contribute 44 percent and the energy sector 45 percent of the republic's industrial output.

LAND AREA

19,400 square miles (50,250 square km), with 336 miles (540 km) of coastline. Arable land makes up 15 percent of the total area.

CURRENCY

1 Russia ruble (RUB) = 100 kopeks
USD 1 = RUB 28.395 (August 2005)
Notes: 10, 50, 100, 500, 1000 rubles
Coins: 1, 2, 5 rubles; 1, 5, 10, 50 kopecks

NATURAL RESOURCES

Oil, natural gas, coal, water. Dagestan produces 310,000 tons of oil and 25,250 million cubic feet (715 million cubic m) of gas per year.

AGRICULTURAL PRODUCTS

Fish, fruit, vegetables

INDUSTRIAL PRODUCTS/ACTIVITY

Chemicals, construction, food products (including wine and brandy), glass, hydroelectric power, large-scale engineering, machinery and tools, shipbuilding, textiles, traditional handicrafts

AIRPORT

Makhachkala

MAJOR PORTS

Makhachkala, Derbent

OIL AND GAS PIPELINES

329 miles (530 km)

ROADS

More than 5,280 miles (8,500 km); at least half are unpaved.

RAILWAYS

About 290 miles (465 km)

HIGHWAYS

Around 190 miles (300 km)

CULTURAL DAGESTAN

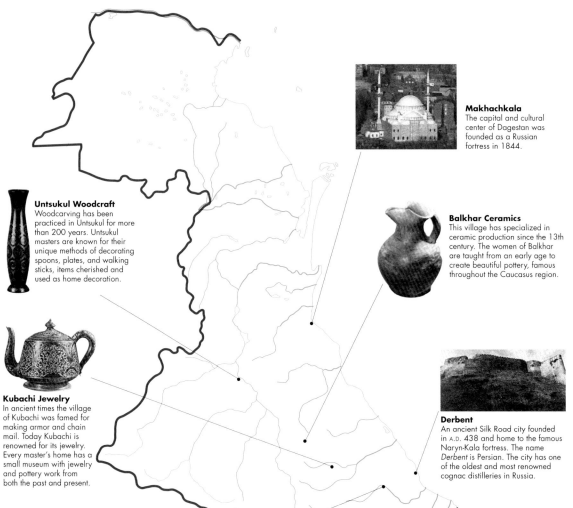

Makhachkala
The capital and cultural center of Dagestan was founded as a Russian fortress in 1844.

Untsukul Woodcraft
Woodcarving has been practiced in Untsukul for more than 200 years. Untsukul masters are known for their unique methods of decorating spoons, plates, and walking sticks, items cherished and used as home decoration.

Balkhar Ceramics
This village has specialized in ceramic production since the 13th century. The women of Balkhar are taught from an early age to create beautiful pottery, famous throughout the Caucasus region.

Kubachi Jewelry
In ancient times the village of Kubachi was famed for making armor and chain mail. Today Kubachi is renowned for its jewelry. Every master's home has a small museum with jewelry and pottery work from both the past and present.

Derbent
An ancient Silk Road city founded in A.D. 438 and home to the famous Naryn-Kala fortress. The name *Derbent* is Persian. The city has one of the oldest and most renowned cognac distilleries in Russia.

Khuchni Carpets
The carpet industry made Khuchni famous across the region. For centuries, thin, light carpets with different shapes and themes, mostly in blue and red, have been part of any Dagestani home.

ABOUT THE CULTURE

OFFICIAL NAME
Republic of Dagestan

POLITICAL STATUS
Constituent subject of the Russian Federation

FLAG
Three horizontal bands in green, blue, and red.

COAT OF ARMS
Round white heraldic shield with a golden eagle in the middle and the sun above. The upper part of the shield has a gold border. The lower part, bordered in blue on the left and in red on the right, shows snowy mountain peaks, a plain, the sea, and a handshake bounded by a green heraldic band with the words "Republic of Dagestan."

CAPITAL
Makhachkala

OTHER CITIES
Derbent, Buynaksk, Izberbash, Kaspiysk, Khasavyurt, Kizilyurt, Kizlyar

POPULATION
2.6 million, or 1.2 percent of the population of the Russian Federation (2002)

ETHNIC GROUPS
Avars 25 percent; Dargins 15 percent; Kumyks 12 percent; Lezgins 11 percent; Russians 11 percent; Laks 5 percent; Azeris 4 percent; Tabasarans 4 percent; Chechens, Nogays, Rutuls, Aguls, Tsakhurs, Tats, Ukrainians, Tatars

RELIGIONS
Islam, Christianity, Judaism. Sunni Muslims make up more than 90 percent of the population.

LANGUAGES
Russian is the official language. In addition, more than 30 local languages are commonly spoken in Dagestan. They include Avar, Dargin, Kumyk, Lezgin, Lak, Azeri, and Tabasaran.

FESTIVALS AND HOLIDAYS
Kurban Bairam, Mavlid, Uraza Bairam, International Women's Day (March 8), Navruz (March 21), Victory Day (May 9), Constitution Day (July 26)

LEADERS IN POLITICS
Magomedali Magomedov—chairman of the State Council since 1994
Atay Aliyev—prime minister since 2004

LEADERS IN THE ARTS
Rasul Gamzatov (poet), Effendi Kapiev (writer), Halilbek Musayasul (painter)

TIME
Greenwich Mean Time plus three hours (GMT + 03:00)

TIME LINE

IN DAGESTAN	IN THE WORLD
	753 B.C. Rome is founded.
End of first millennium B.C. Caucasian Albania, the first big state in the eastern Caucasus, emerges.	**116–17 B.C.** The Roman Empire reaches its greatest extent, under Emperor Trajan (98–17).
Third century A.D. Sasanids of Persia invade the southern part of what is now Dagestan.	
Fourth century Huns capture the coastline to the north of Derbent.	
Fifth century Sizable cities emerge, most notably Derbent (438 A.D.), Semender, Kubachi.	
	A.D. 600 Height of Mayan civilization
664–914 Dagestan is subject to repeated invasions by the Arabs.	
11th century Seljuks capture what is now Azerbaijan and part of Dagestan.	**1000** The Chinese perfect gunpowder and begin to use it in warfare.
1220 Dagestan is invaded by the Mongols.	**1530** Beginning of transatlantic slave trade organized by the Portuguese in Africa.
mid-1500s Russians enter the Caucasus; the first serious interactions between Dagestani tribes and Russians begin.	**1558–1603** Reign of Elizabeth I of England **1620** Pilgrims sail the *Mayflower* to America.
1722 Peter the Great invades Persia and the eastern Caucasus.	**1776** U.S. Declaration of Independence
1700s Russia establishes a stronghold along the Terek River.	**1789–99** The French Revolution

IN DAGESTAN	IN THE WORLD
1813 The Russians and Persians sign the Gulistan Peace Treaty. Persia cedes the khanates along the Caspian Sea to Russia.	
1817–64 The Caucasian War between northern Caucasian mountain tribes and Russia	**1861** The U.S. Civil War begins.
	1869 The Suez Canal is opened.
	1914 World War I begins.
1917 Revolution in Russia	
1921 The Autonomous Republic of Dagestan established by the Bolshevik government	**1939** World War II begins.
	1945 The United States drops atomic bombs on Hiroshima and Nagasaki.
	1949 The North Atlantic Treaty Organization (NATO) is formed.
	1957 The Russians launch Sputnik.
	1966–69 The Chinese Cultural Revolution
	1986 Nuclear power disaster at Chernobyl in Ukraine
1991 Dagestan declares itself a sovereign republic within the Russian Federation.	**1991** Break-up of the Soviet Union
1994–96 The first Chechen war. Chechen militants invade Dagestan in an attempt to establish a Muslim state.	**1997** Hong Kong is returned to China.
	2001 Terrorists crash planes in New York, Washington, D.C., and Pennsylvania.
	2003 War in Iraq

GLOSSARY

adat
A set of customary laws.

ajam
An alphabet based on Arabic script.

aoul (ah-OOL)
A village.

dzhigit
A rider; figuratively, it means a deft, brave man.

farmingo (fahr-MEEN-goh)
A trick performed by rope walkers.

gazavat
In Islam, armed defense or struggle against the unfaithful.

godekan (ghoh-deh-KAHN)
A village square, usually with a mosque. The center of communication and socializing for men living in rural areas.

hajj
A journey to Mecca for religious purposes that all Muslims try to make at least once in their lifetimes.

jamaat (jah-mah-AHT)
A rural community.

lezginka (lez-GHEEN-ka)
A famous Dagestani dance.

madrassa
A middle school run by a mosque.

mullah
A Muslim teacher of law and religion.

nakshbandia
The Sufi order that played a crucial role in Dagestan's conversion to Islam.

namus (nah-MOOS)
Core of the ethical and moral code of Dagestan. *Namus* stands for support, sympathy, and the ability to give.

papakha (pah-PAH-khah)
A tall astrakhan hat.

sharia
A system of religious laws followed by Muslims.

tuhum
A clan comprising all relatives on the paternal side.

umra
A short pilgrimage made by Muslims.

yag' (YAKH)
Masculinity. The behavioral code informing Dagestani concepts of manhood and including nobility, gentleness, hard work, generosity, respect to the elderly, honor, courage, and charity toward the weak and the poor.

FURTHER INFORMATION

BOOKS

Blanch, Leslie. *The Sabres of Paradise*. New York: Carroll & Graf Publishers, Inc., 1984.

Chenciner, Robert. *Daghestan: Tradition and Survival*. New York: St. Martin's Press, 1997.

Griffin, Nicholas. *Caucasus: Mountain Men and Holy Wars*. New York: Thomas Dunne Books, 2003.

Kennan, George. *Vagabond Life: The Caucasus Journals of George Kennan*. Seattle, WA: University of Washington Press, 2003.

WEB SITES

The Archaeological Research Facility Newsletter: Excavations in Daghestan.
  http://sscl.berkeley.edu/arf/newsletter/3.2/daghestan.html

BBC News Country Profiles: Regions and Territories: Dagestan.
  http://news.bbc.co.uk/2/hi/europe/country_profiles/3659904.stm

Central Asia and the Caucasus: Journal of Social and Political Studies (articles on the political situation in the region). www.ca-c.org/dataeng/bd_eng.shtml

Center for Russian Nature Conservation: Dagestansky Zapovednik.
  www.wild-russia.org/bioregion3/Dagestansky/3_dagest.htm

Fragilecologies: Central Asia (articles on environmental issues in the region).
  www.fragilecologies.com/asia.html

Jozan: Daghestan Rugs and Carpets, Photo Gallery. www.jozan.net/distrikter/daghestan.asp

NUPI Centre for Russian Studies: Administrative Units: Dagestan.
  www.nupi.no/cgi-win/Russland/a_enhet.exe?DAGESTAN

Paintings by Halilbek Musayasul.
  http://kafkasyagrubu.org/kafkasyali_ressamlar/halil_bek_musayyasul

People's Poet of Daghestan Rasul Gamzatov. www.gamzatov.ru/bioeng.html

The Red Book fo the Peoples of the Russian empire. www.eki.ee/books/redbook

Wikipedia: Dagestan. http://en.wikipedia.org/wiki/Dagestan

MUSIC

Ay Lazzat (Oh Pleasure): Songs and Melodies from Dagestan. Pan Records, 1995.

BIBLIOGRAPHY

Antonchikov, A. N., et al. "Desertification and Ecological Problems of Pasture Stockbreeding in the Steppe Regions of Southern Russia." IUCN – The World Conservation Union Office for Russia and CIS. Moscow, 2002.

Dobaev, Igor. "Jihad in the Islamic World and the Northern Caucasus—Theory and Practice." *Central Asia and the Caucasus*, no. 1 (25) (2004): 71–78.

Gammer, Moshe. "Walking the Tightrope Between Nationalism(s) and Islam(s): The Case of Daghestan." *Central Asian Survey* 21, no. 2 (June 2002): 133–142.

"Granitsa Rossii budet prokhodit po pravomu beregu Dona esli ne udastsia vyrabotat normalnuyu kavkazskuyu politiku." Segodnia, September 7, 1999.

Meskhidze, Julietta. "Imam Shaykh Mansur: A Few Stanzas to a Familiar Portrait." *Central Asian Survey* 21, no. 3 (September 2002): 301–324.

"Moscow props up Dagestan's 2004 budget." BBC Monitoring, February 17, 2004.

Murtuzaliev, Sergei. "Ethnopolitical Processes in the Northern Caucasus and Their Assessment by the Population." *Central Asia and the Caucasus*, no. 3 (27) (2004): 98–105.

Tsapieva, Olga. "Post-Soviet Socioeconomic Development in Daghestan." *Central Asia and the Caucasus*, no. 2 (8) (2001): 168–176.

Ware, Robert Bruce, and Enver Kisriev. "Prospects for Political Stability and Economic Development in Dagestan." *Central Asian Survey* 21, no. 2 (June 2002): 143–156.

Ware, Robert Bruce, Enver Kisriev, Werner Patzelt, and Ute Roericht. "Stability in the Caucasus: The Perspective from Dagestan." *Problems of Post-Communism* 50, 2 (March/April 2003).

Wieczynski, Joseph L., ed. *The Modern Encyclopedia of Russian and Soviet History*. Gulf Breeze, FL: Academic International Press, 1978.

INDEX